The Fabulous Adult Coloring Book of Modern Geometric Art Designs for Art-Loving/Coloring Fanatics

By Michael "Dean" Barr

Copyright ©2018 Michael Barr
Book design by Jane Font
Edited by Vince Font
Published by Glass Spider Publishing
www.glassspiderpublishing.com
ISBN 978-0-9997070-6-7

This coloring book is dedicated to my wife Cyndi. She is and has always been the biggest supporter of my artwork, and my best friend! And special thanks to our very good friends Vince and Jane Font at Glass Spider Publishing for their outstanding professional services. Their extensive experience and personal insights were invaluable in getting this coloring book professionally prepared for publishing.

The images in this coloring book reflect the drawings (doodles, actually) I create during the many meetings I attend as a program manager for an aerospace manufacturing and engineering company. Drawing alongside my notes during these sometimes very lengthy meetings helps me stay focused.

All drawings are done in pen and ink and are best described as modern geometric shapes based on the basic drawing elements of lines, circles, and squares. When I start a new drawing, I have no preconceived idea of what I want to create; I just follow my intuition. The drawings are usually about 1" to 2" square, depending on how long the meeting lasts.

Later, I scan my favorites into Adobe Illustrator and create vector files that I can use to repeat the original drawing and create complex patterns. Doing this is a lot of fun, as the images can take on a life of their own, creating patterns that I never envisioned while creating the original.

Over the years, I've looked for ways to be able to share these drawings with others. Recently, a friend suggested making a coloring book. I thought this was a fantastic idea, and this book is the result of bringing to life that suggestion.

Both original individual designs and design patterns are displayed in the pages of this book. My intent in creating this book was to spark your imagination and to see how you can better the pages by adding your unique interpretations to the design. Have fun adding color and, if it suits you, additional color patterns to the images within!

Note: There are two extra blank pages in this book. One of them can be used to test your media to see how it reacts to the paper. The other is to be removed from the book and used as a backing page to prevent possible bleed-through from affecting the image behind the one you're coloring.

Test your media on this page

Remove this page to use as a backing

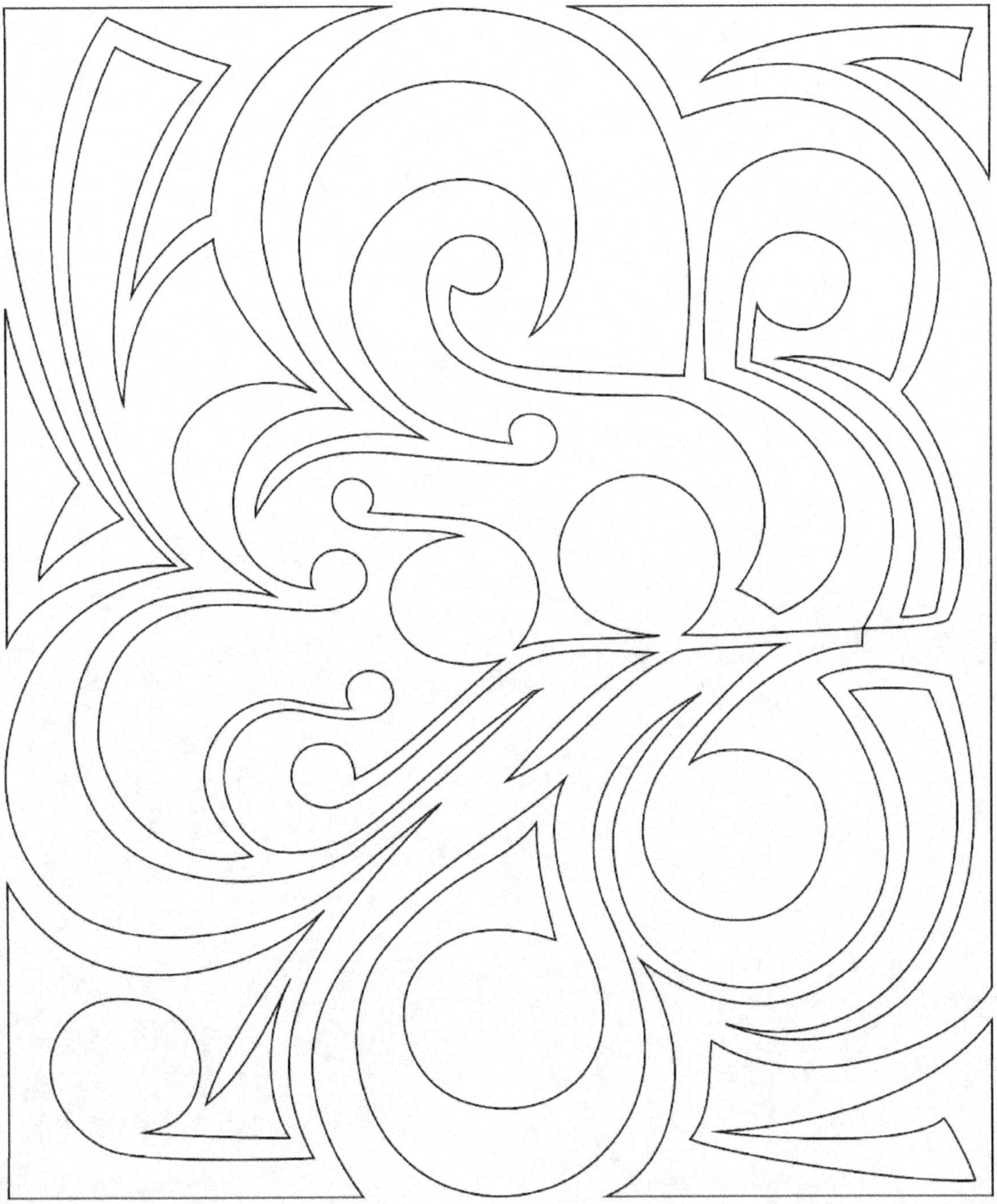

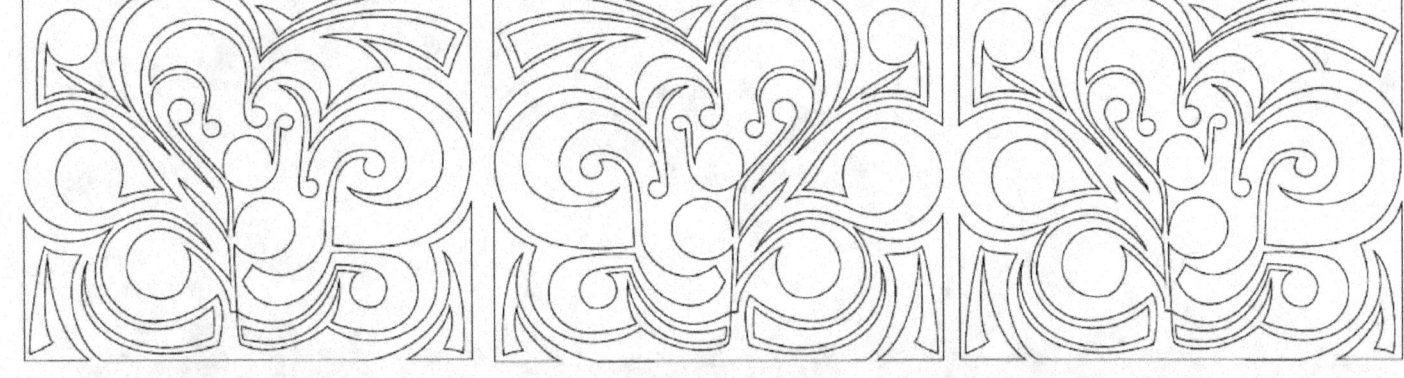

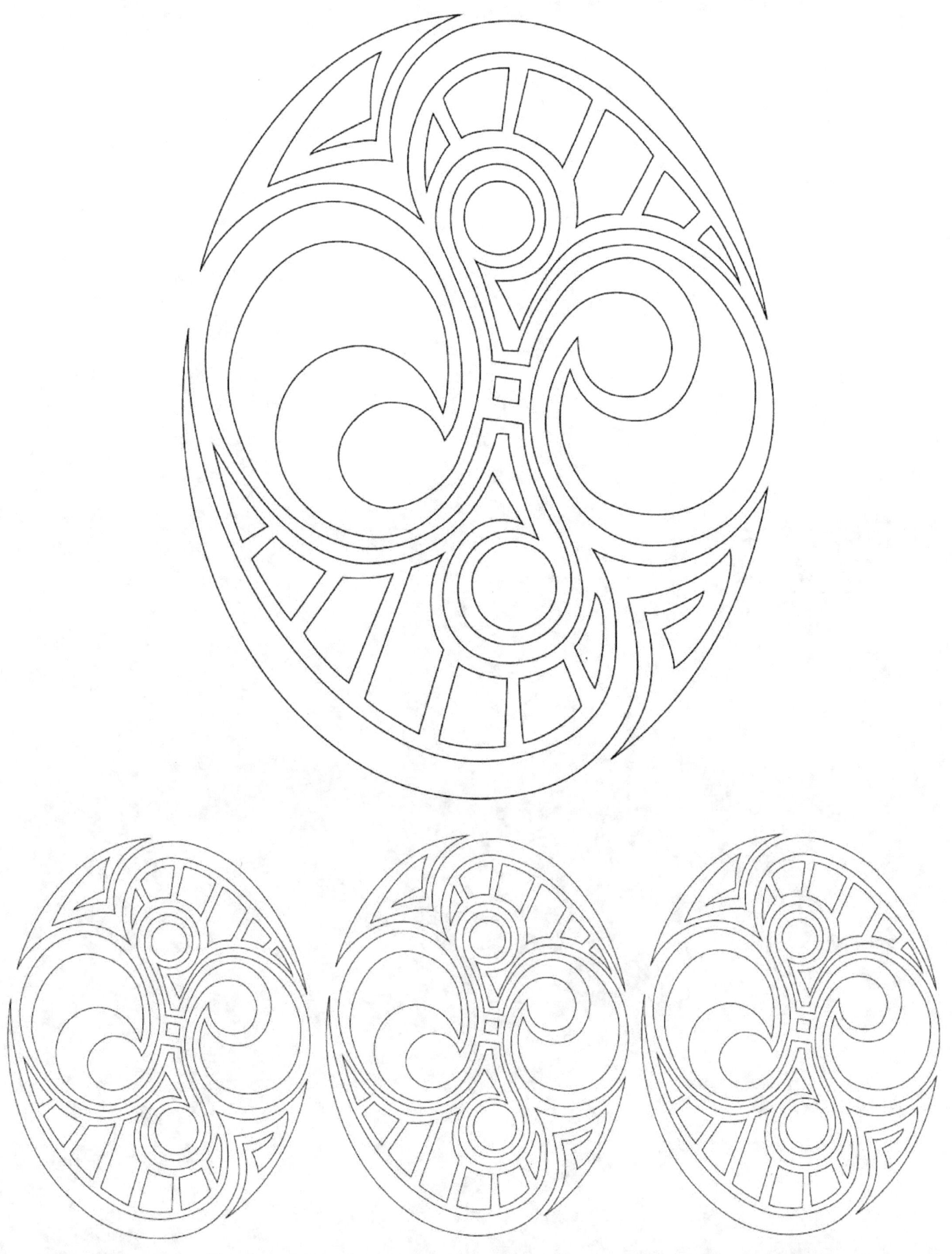

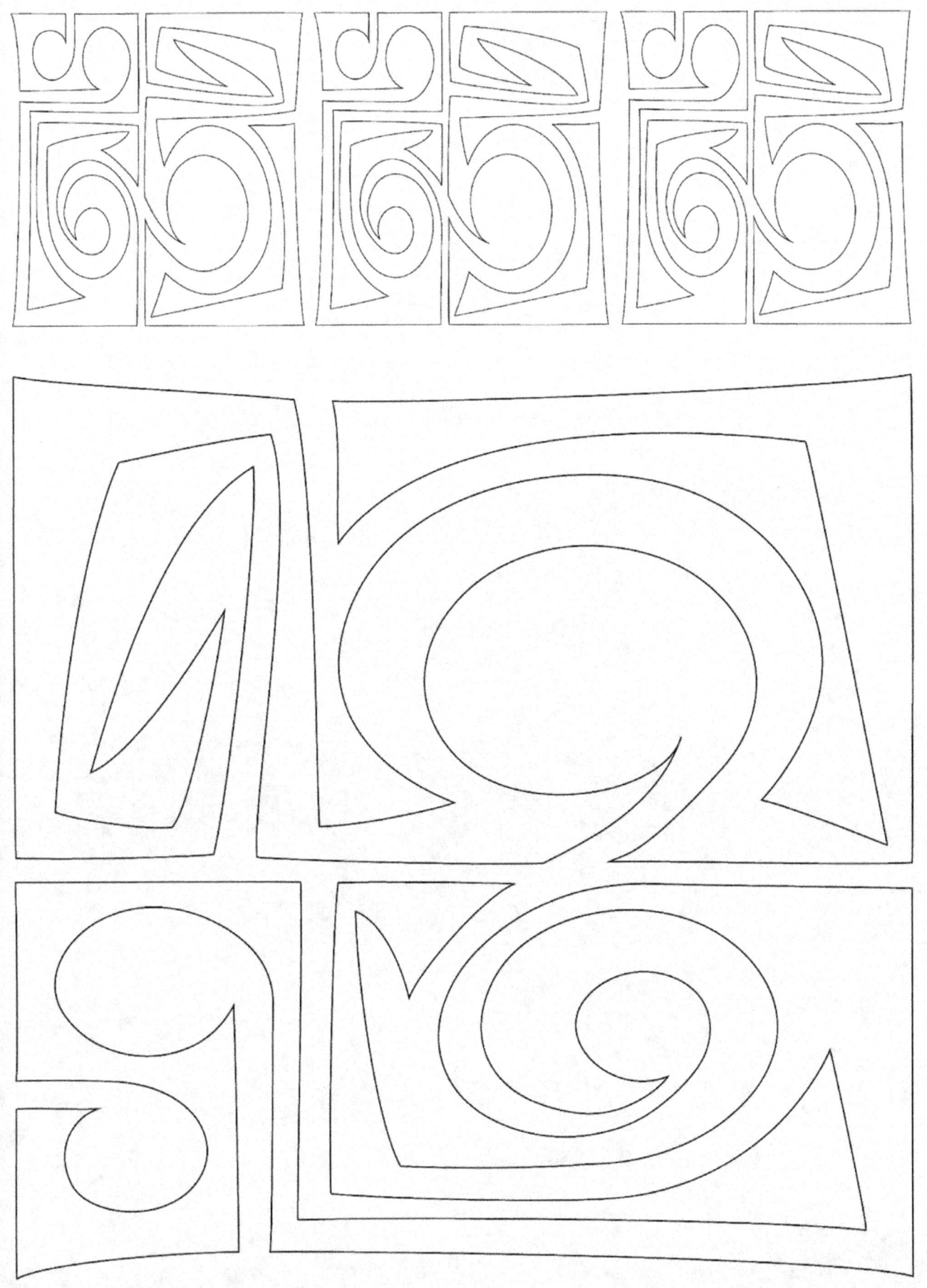

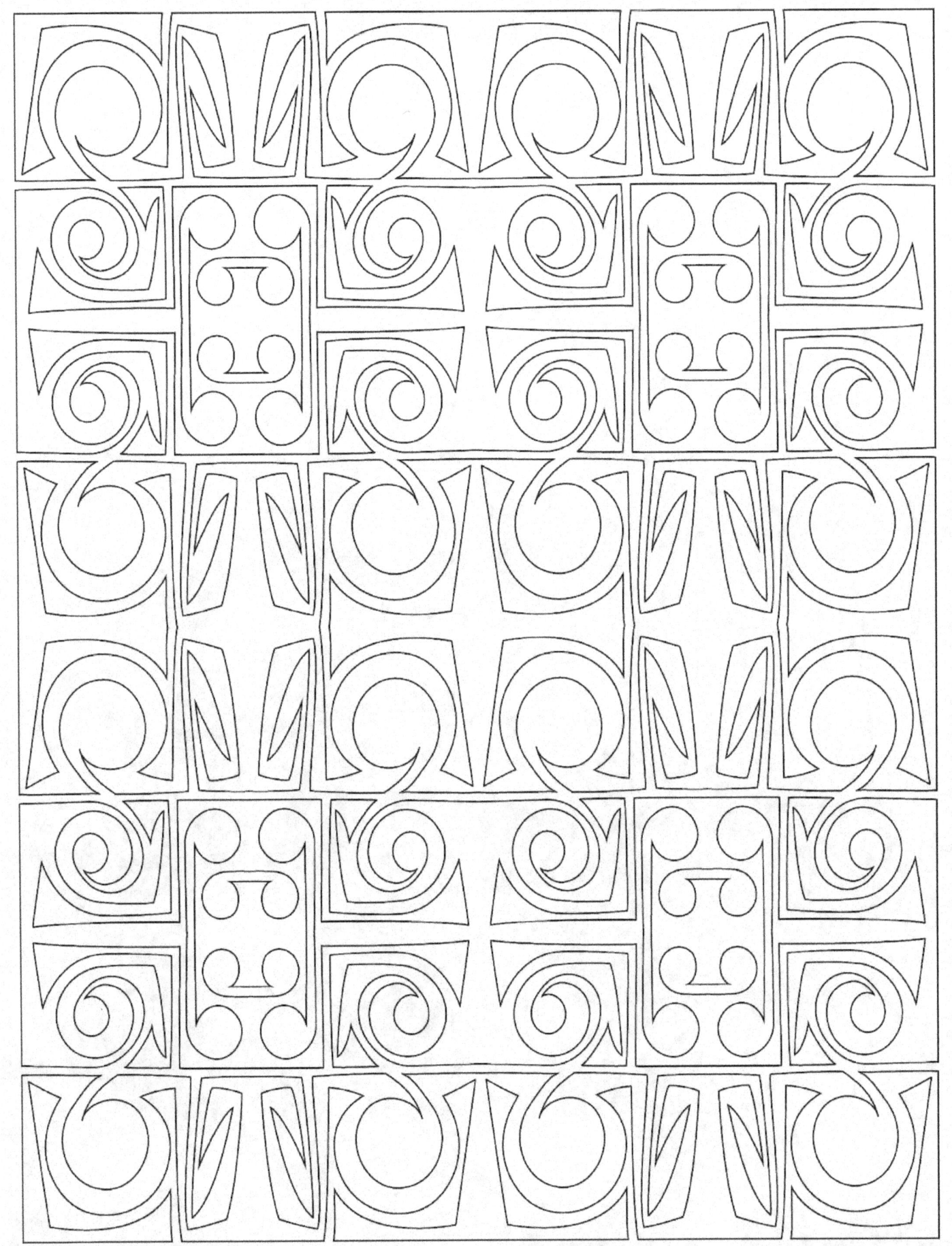

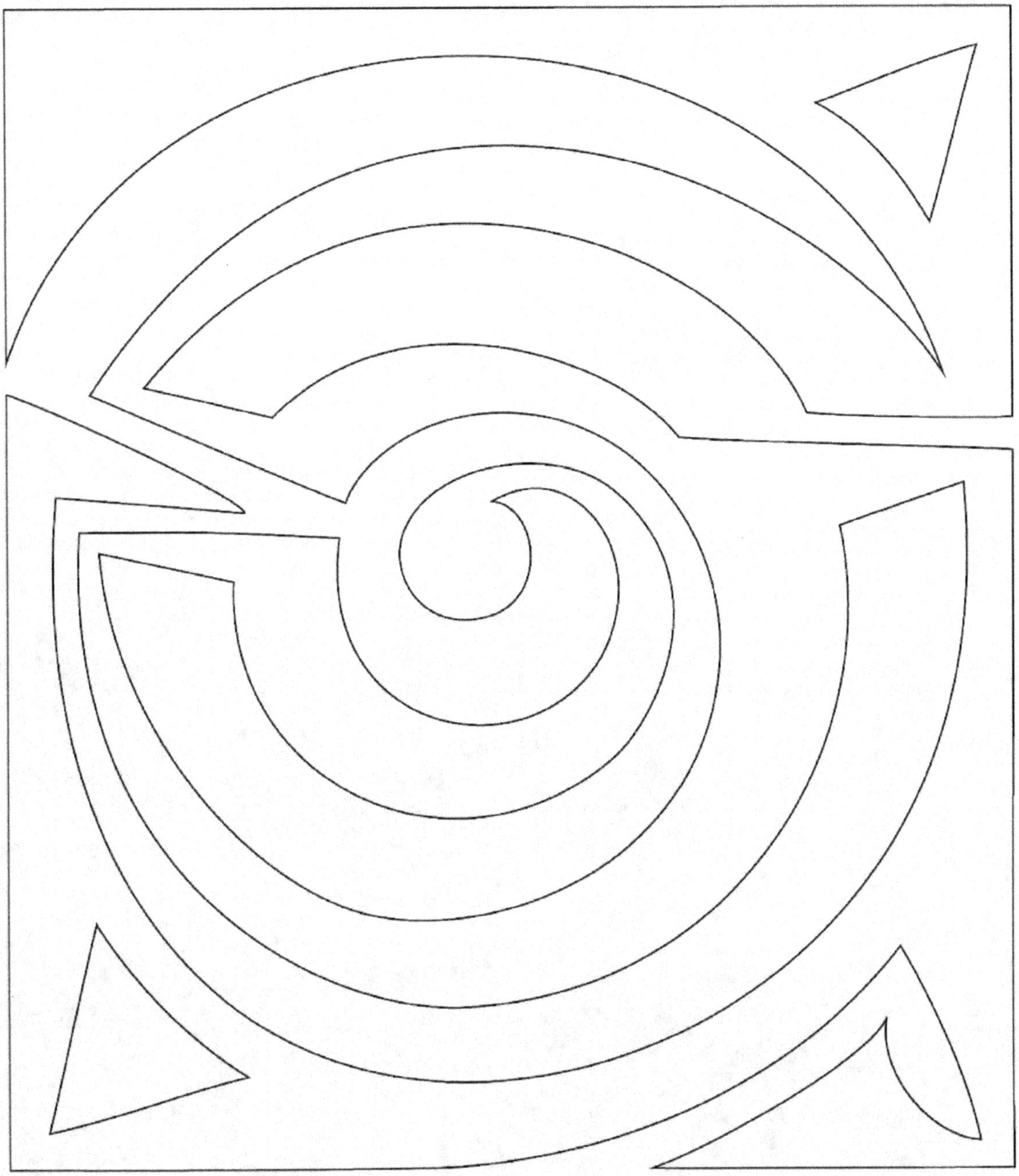

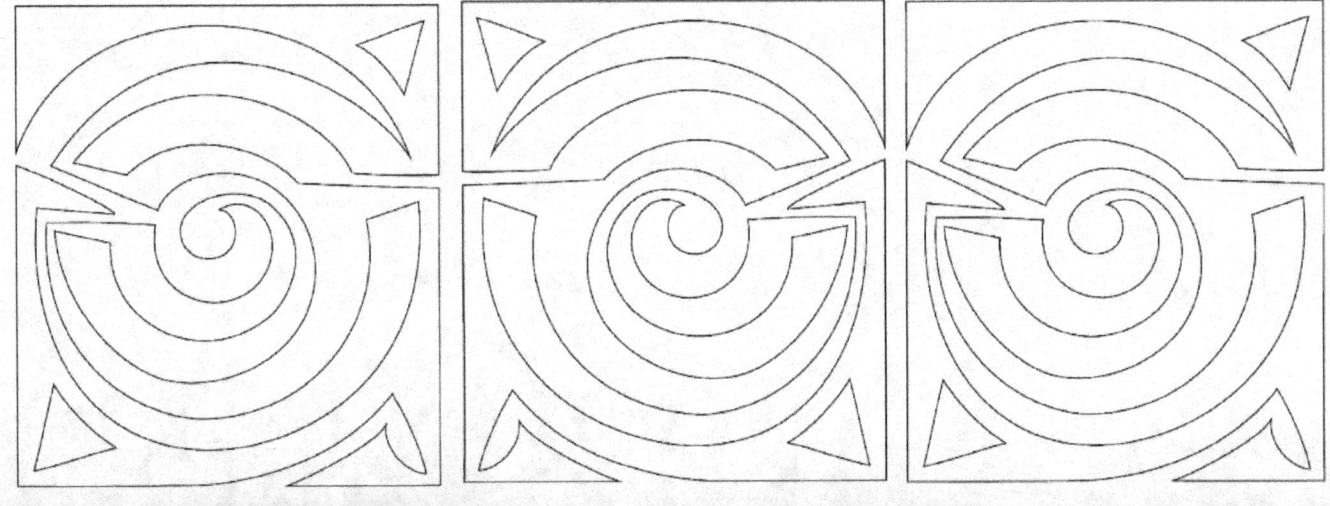

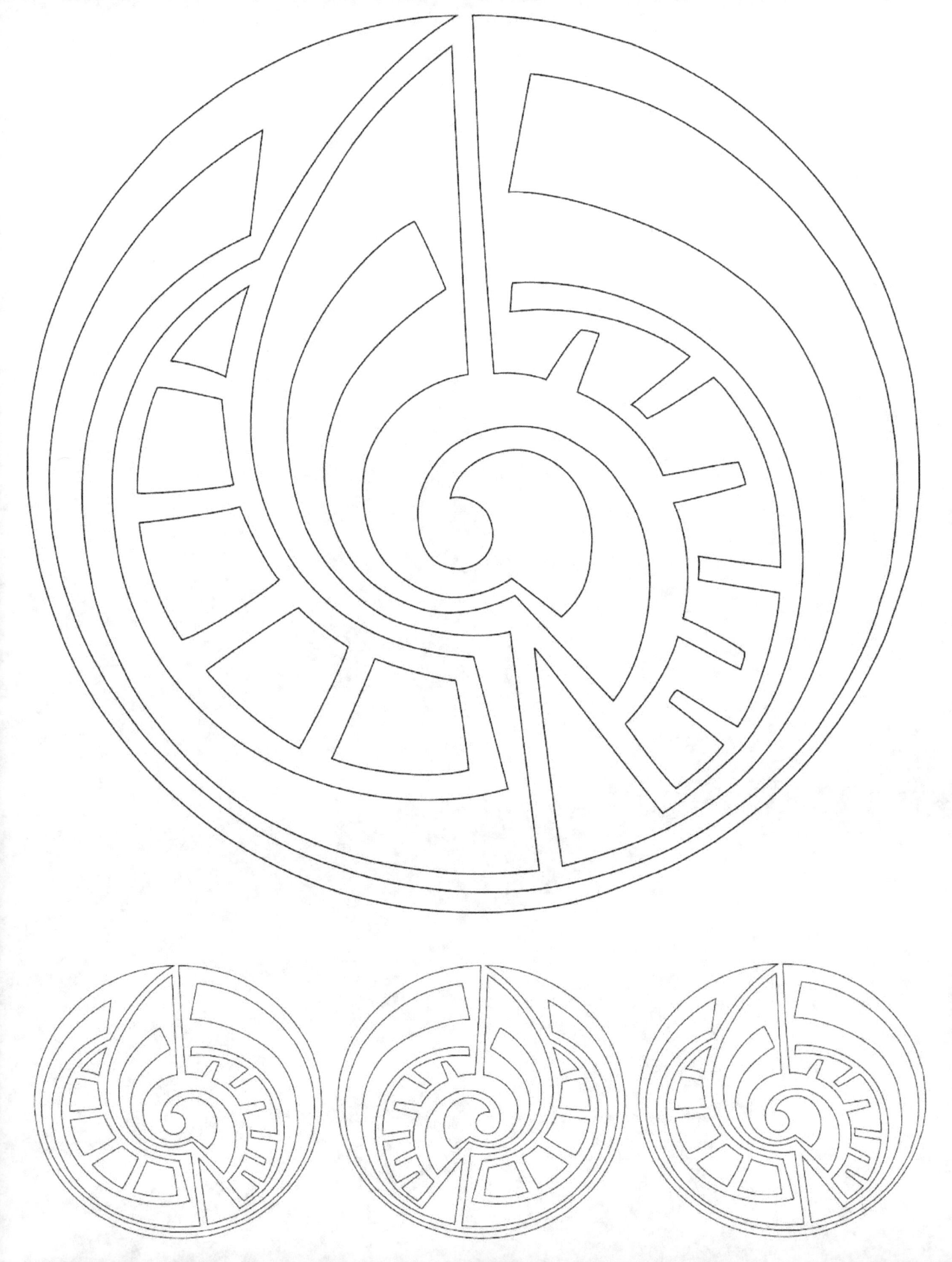

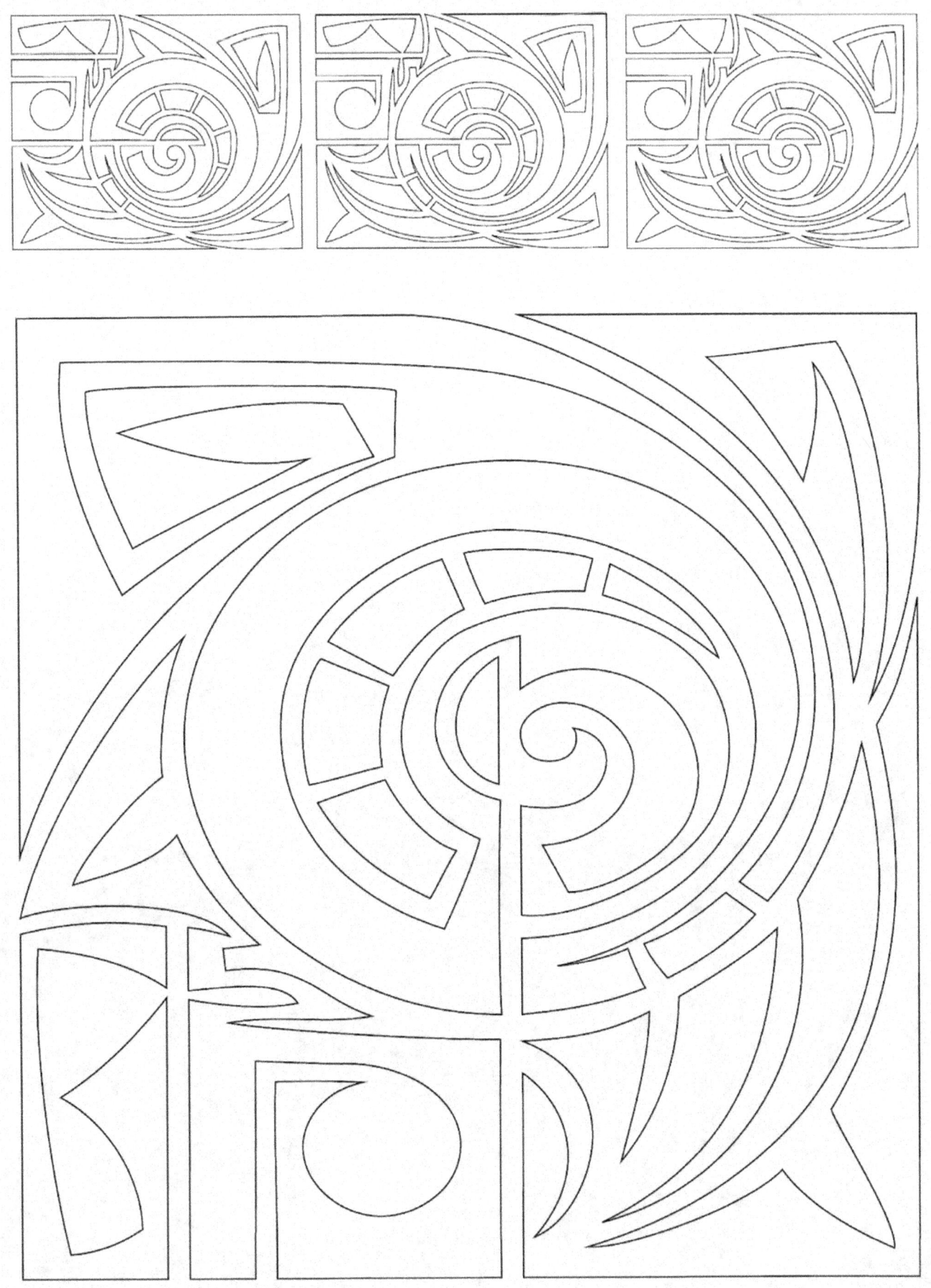

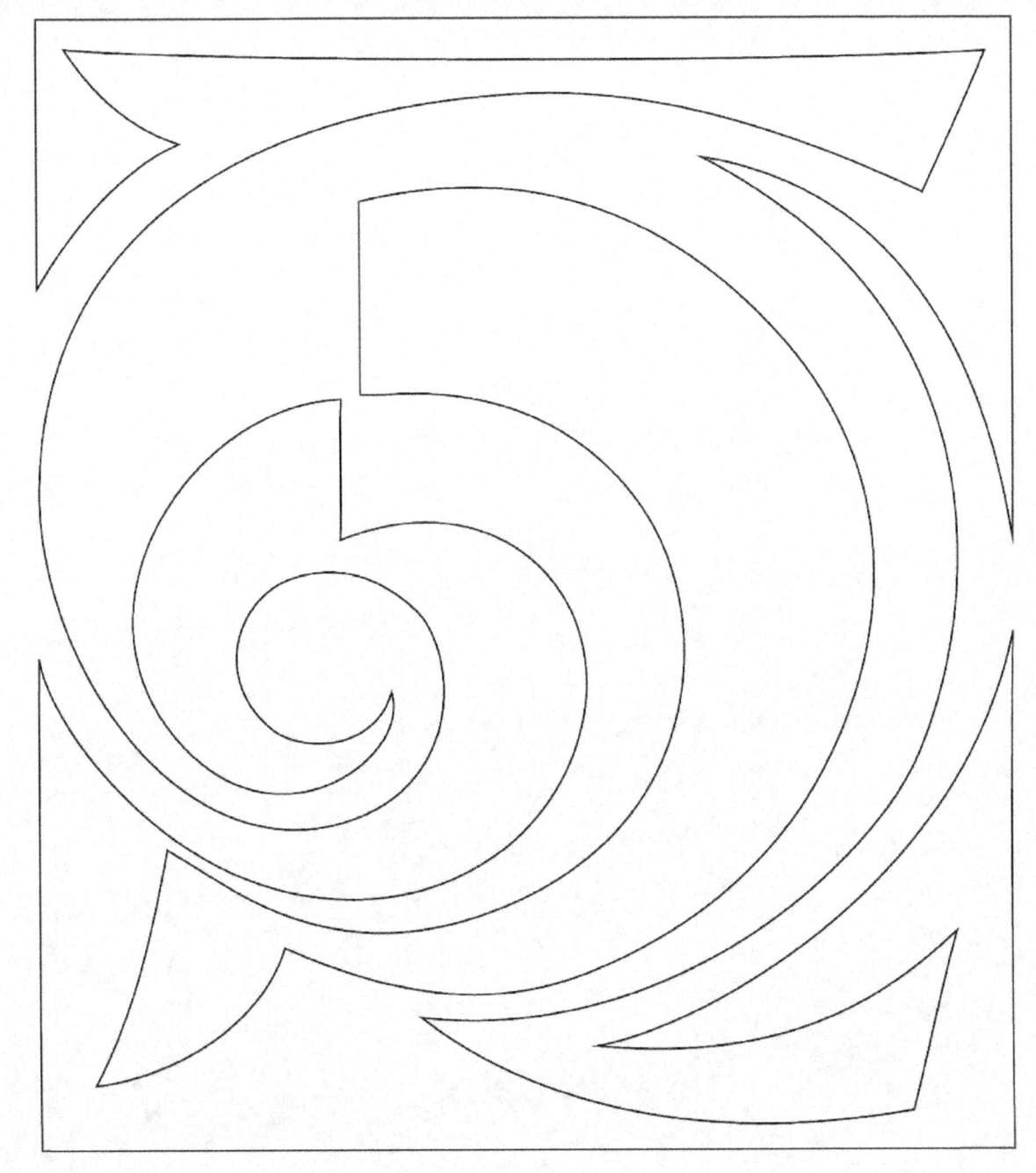

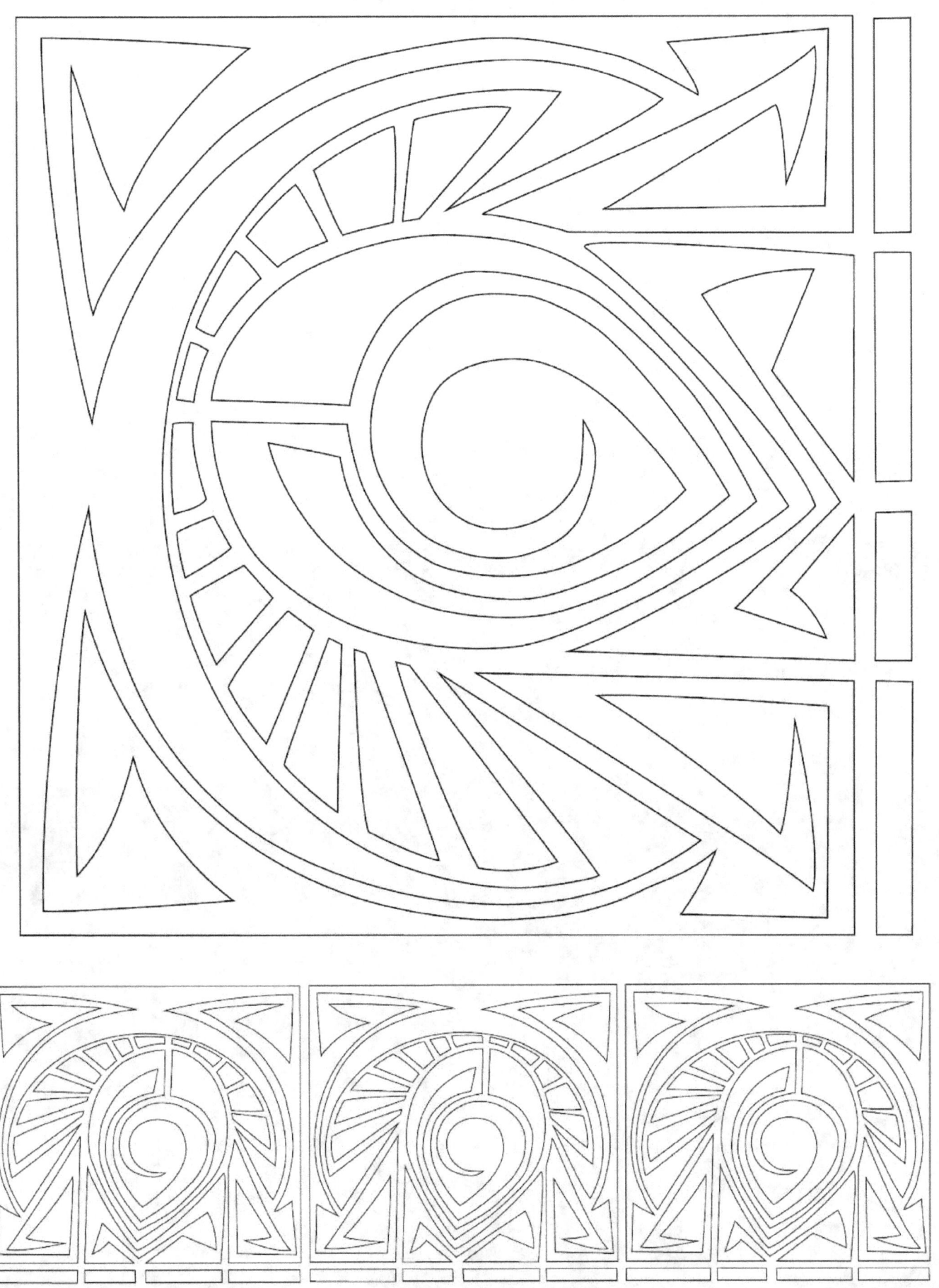

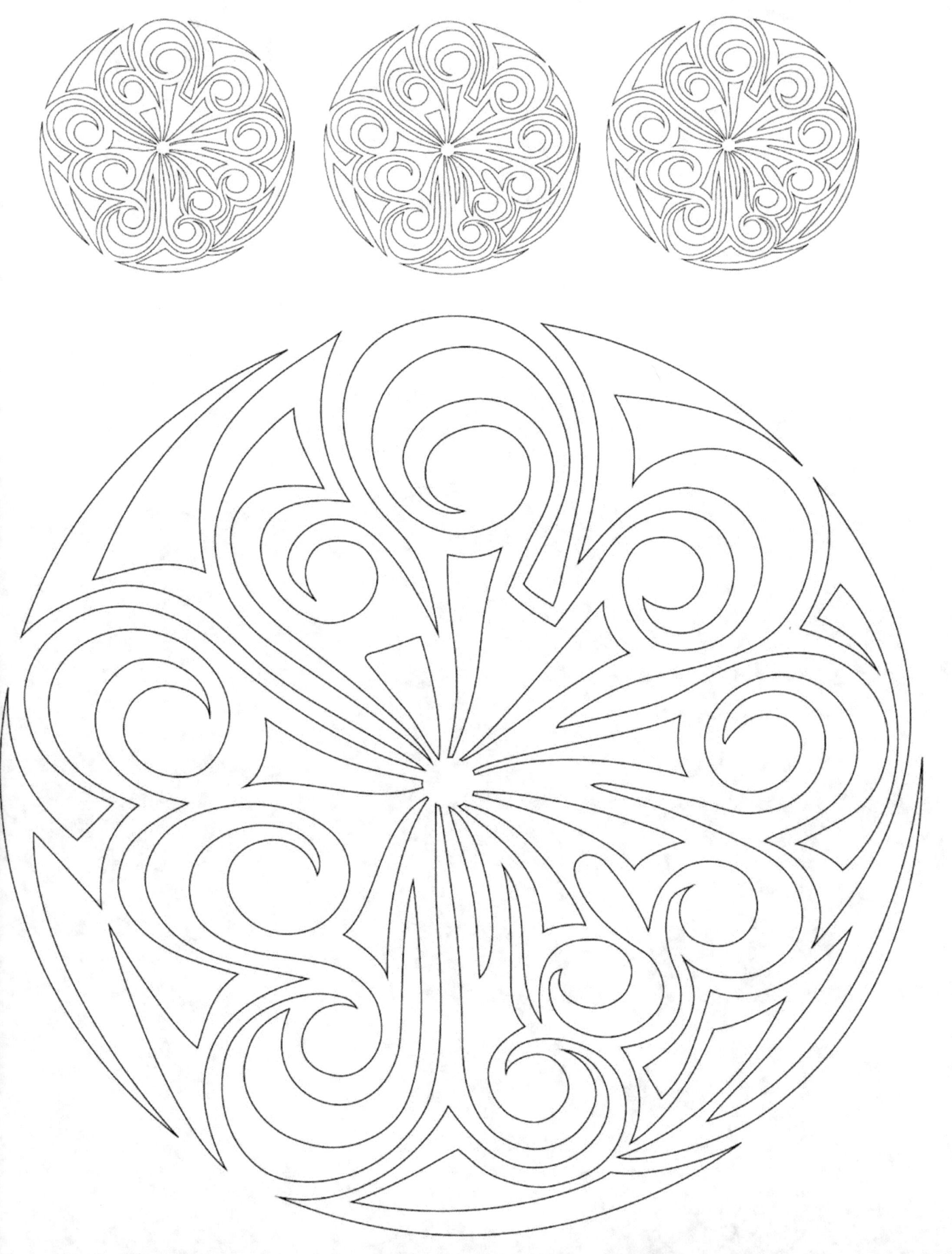

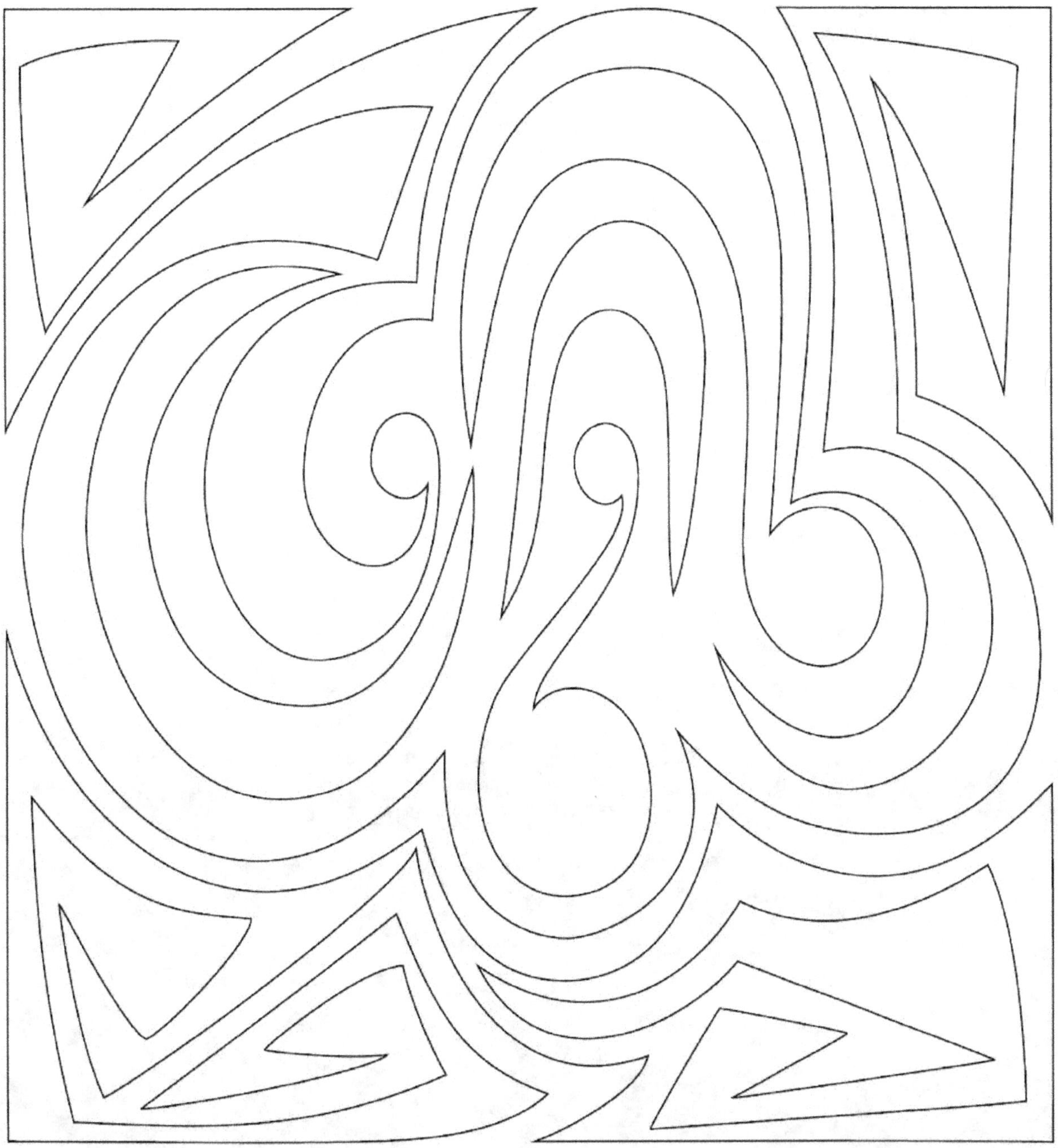

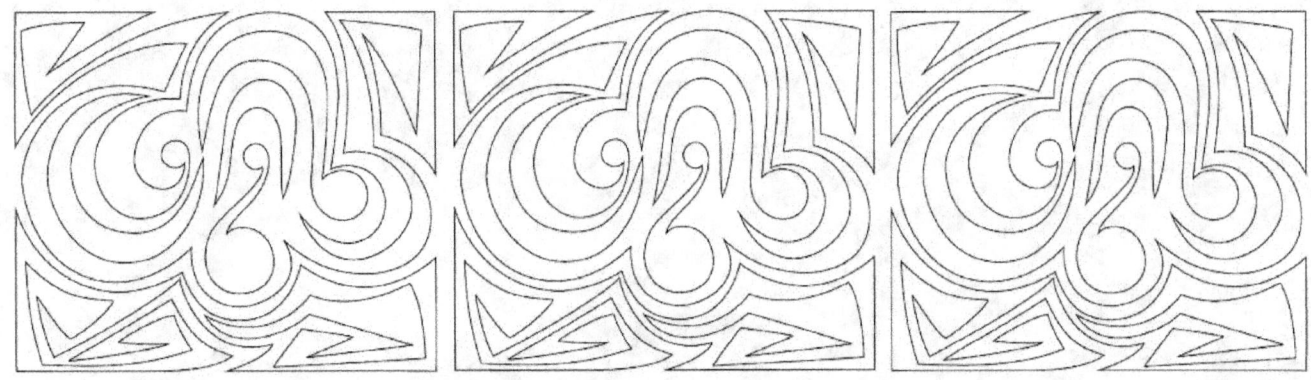

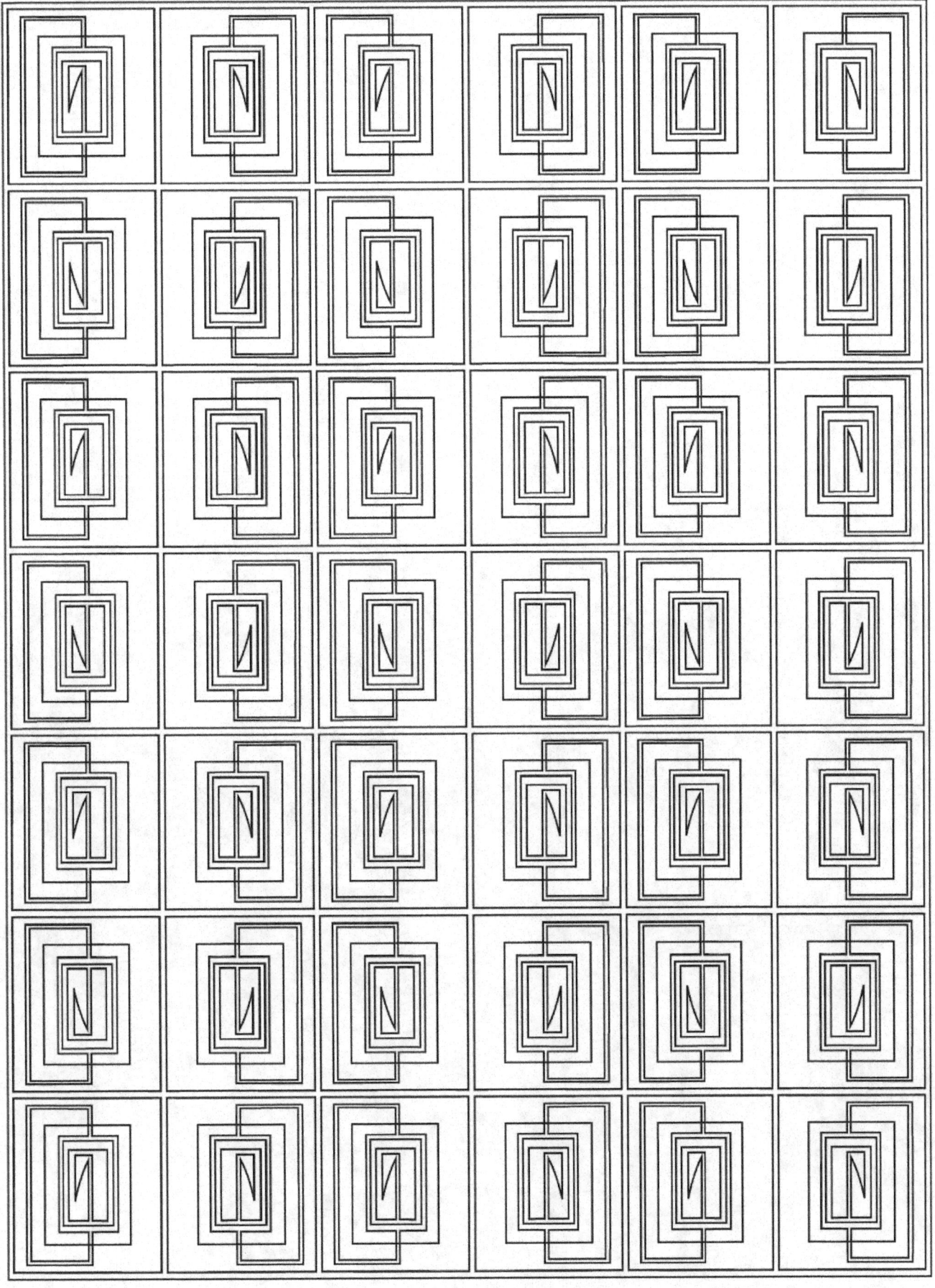

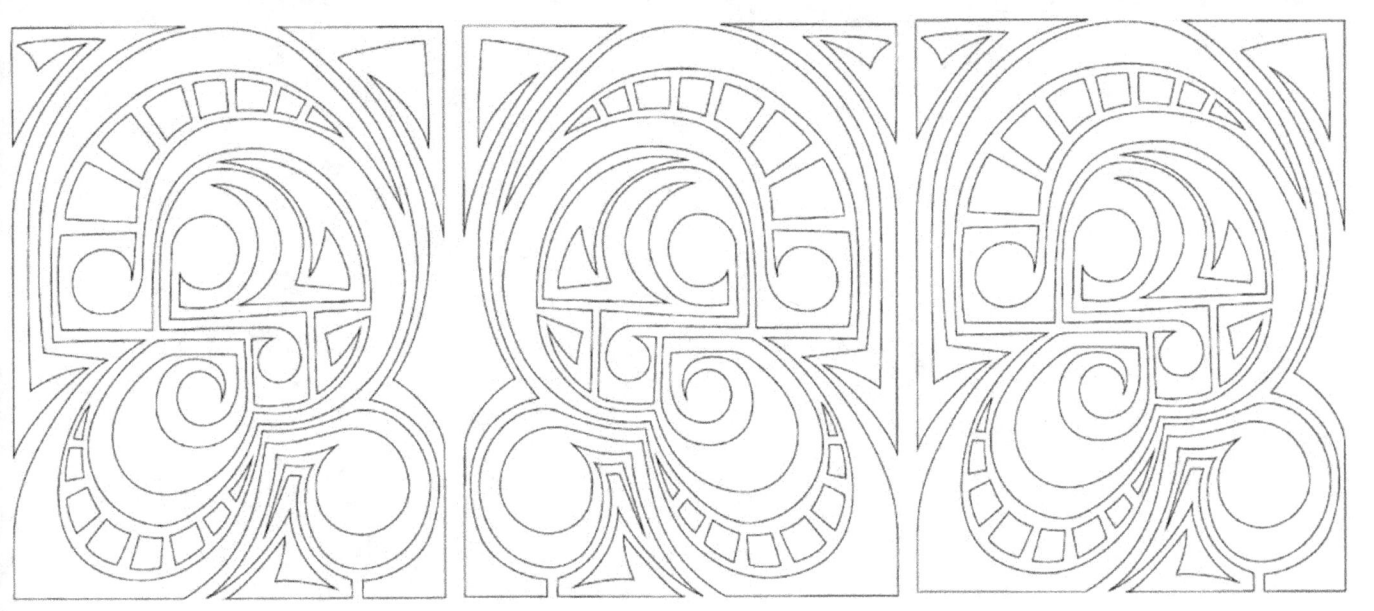

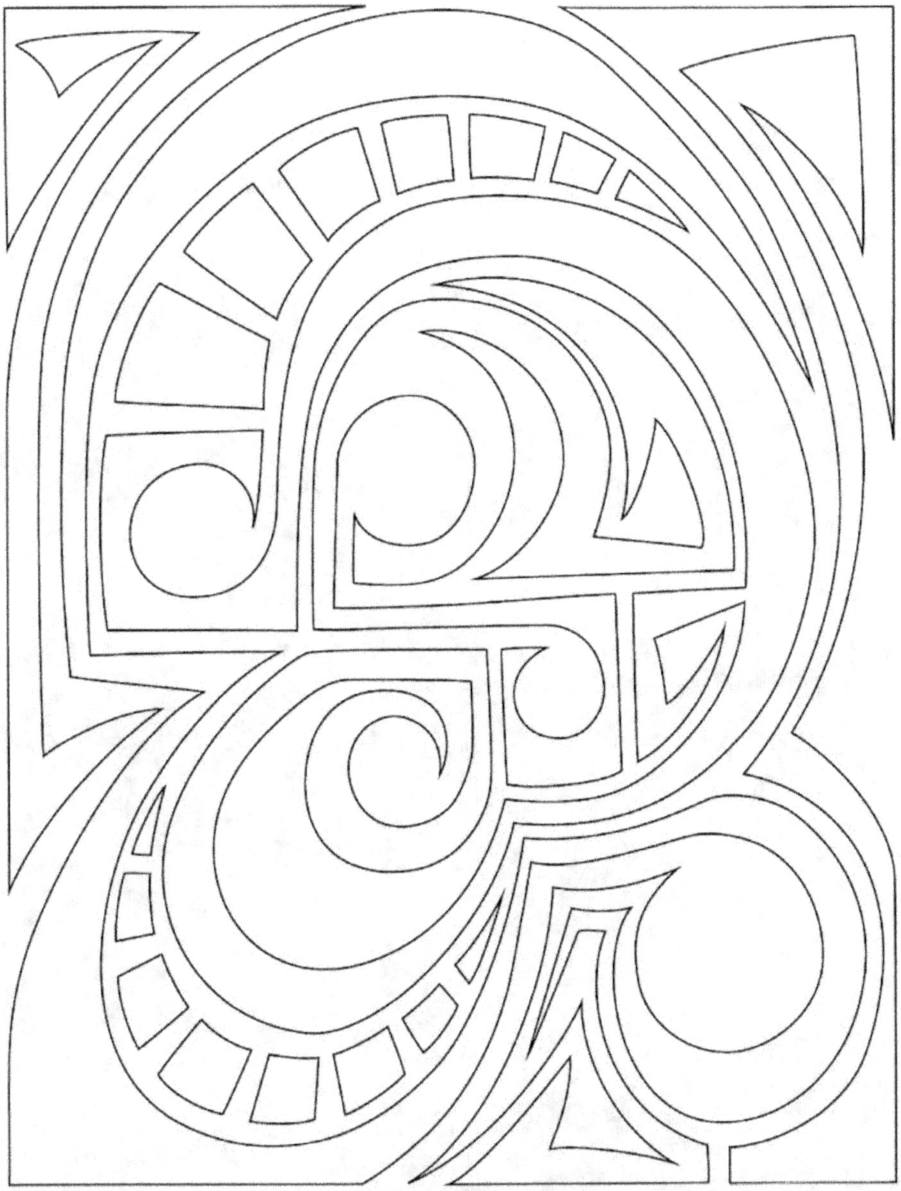

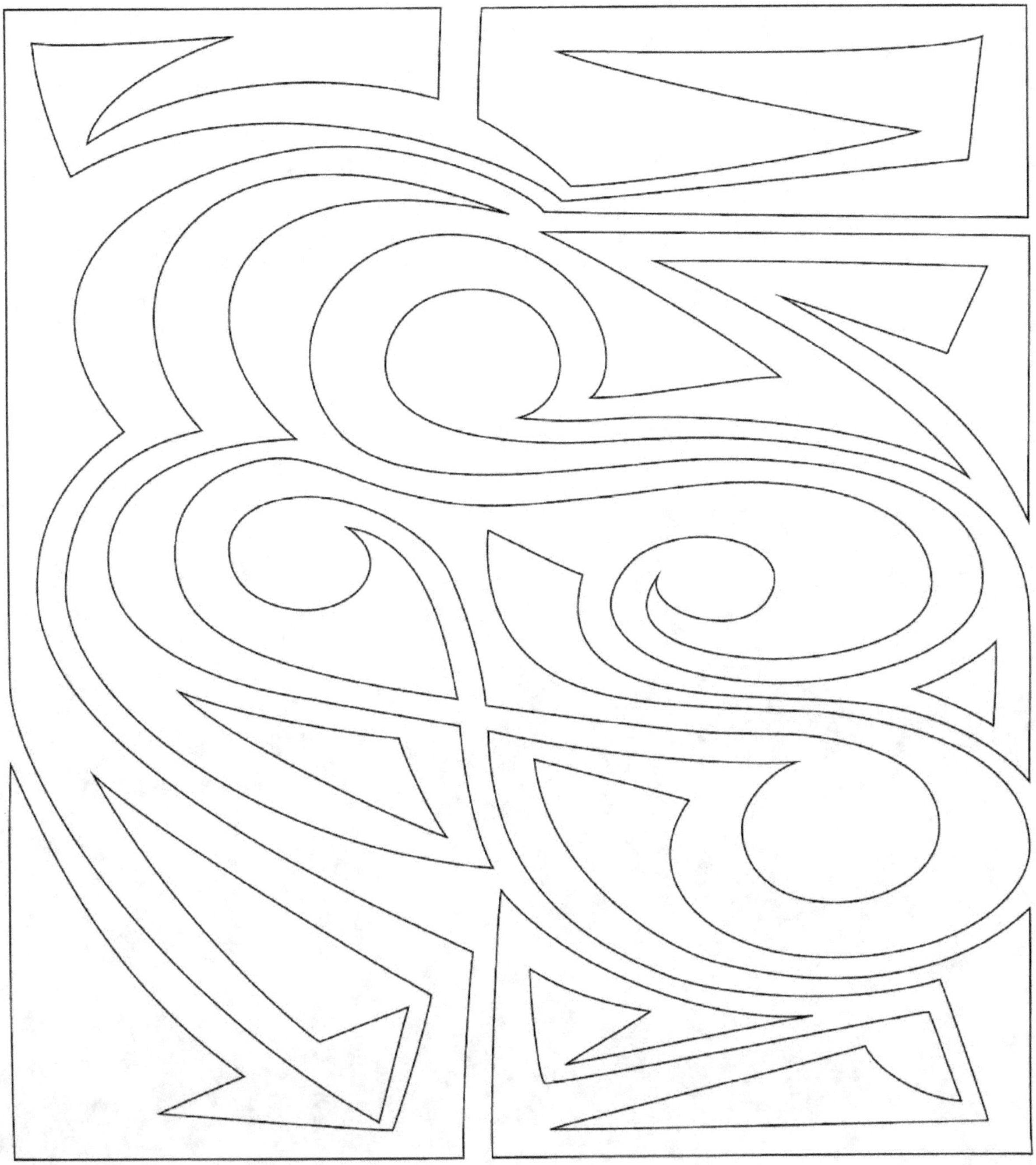

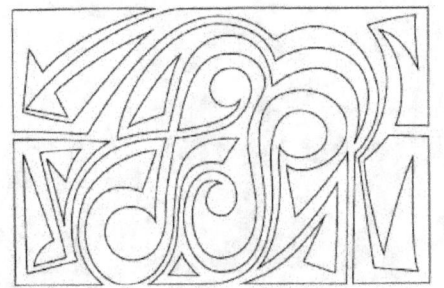
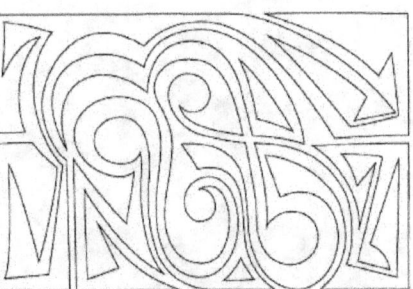
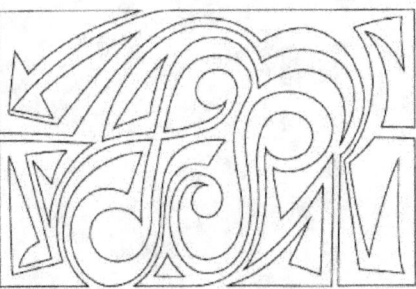

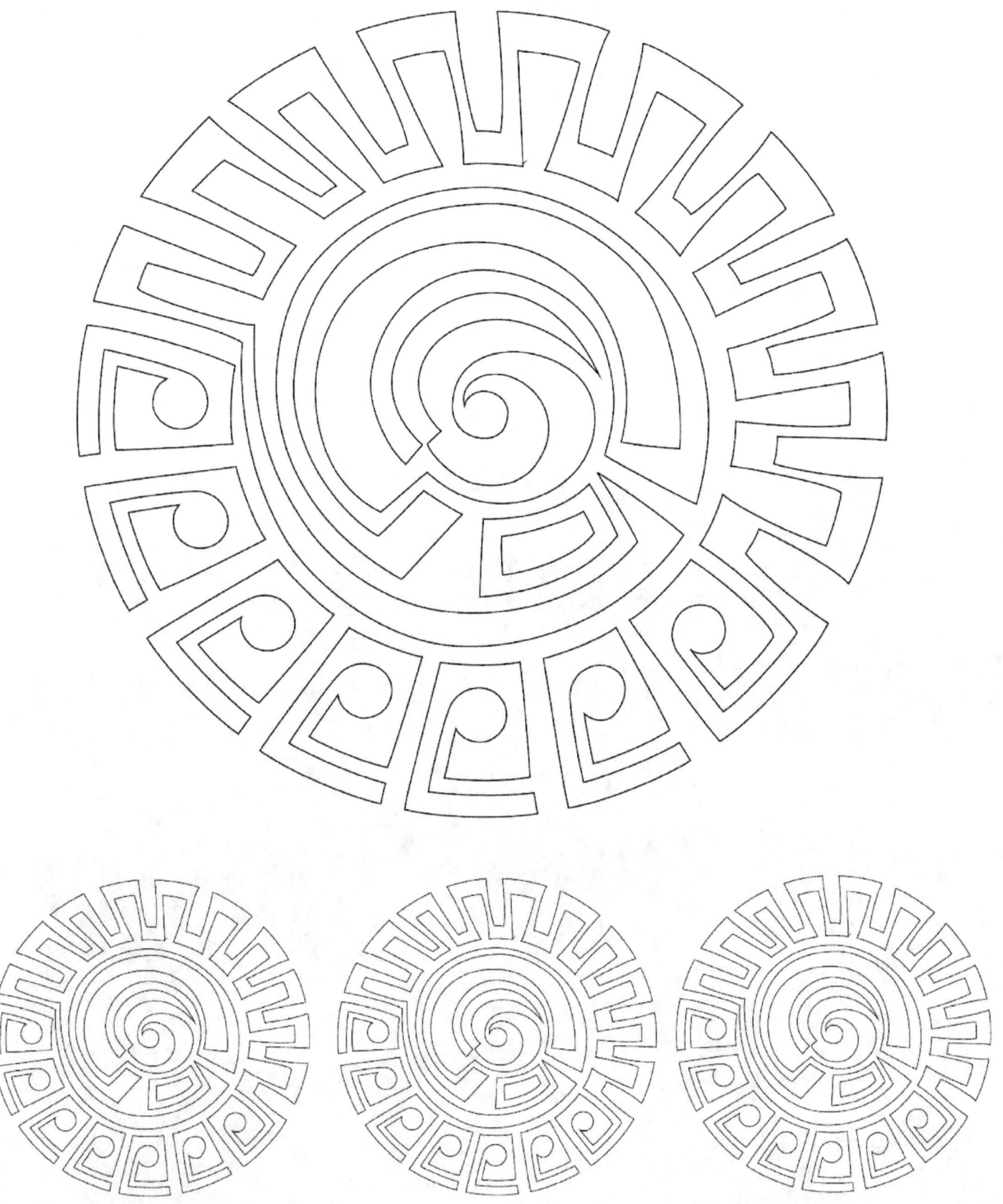

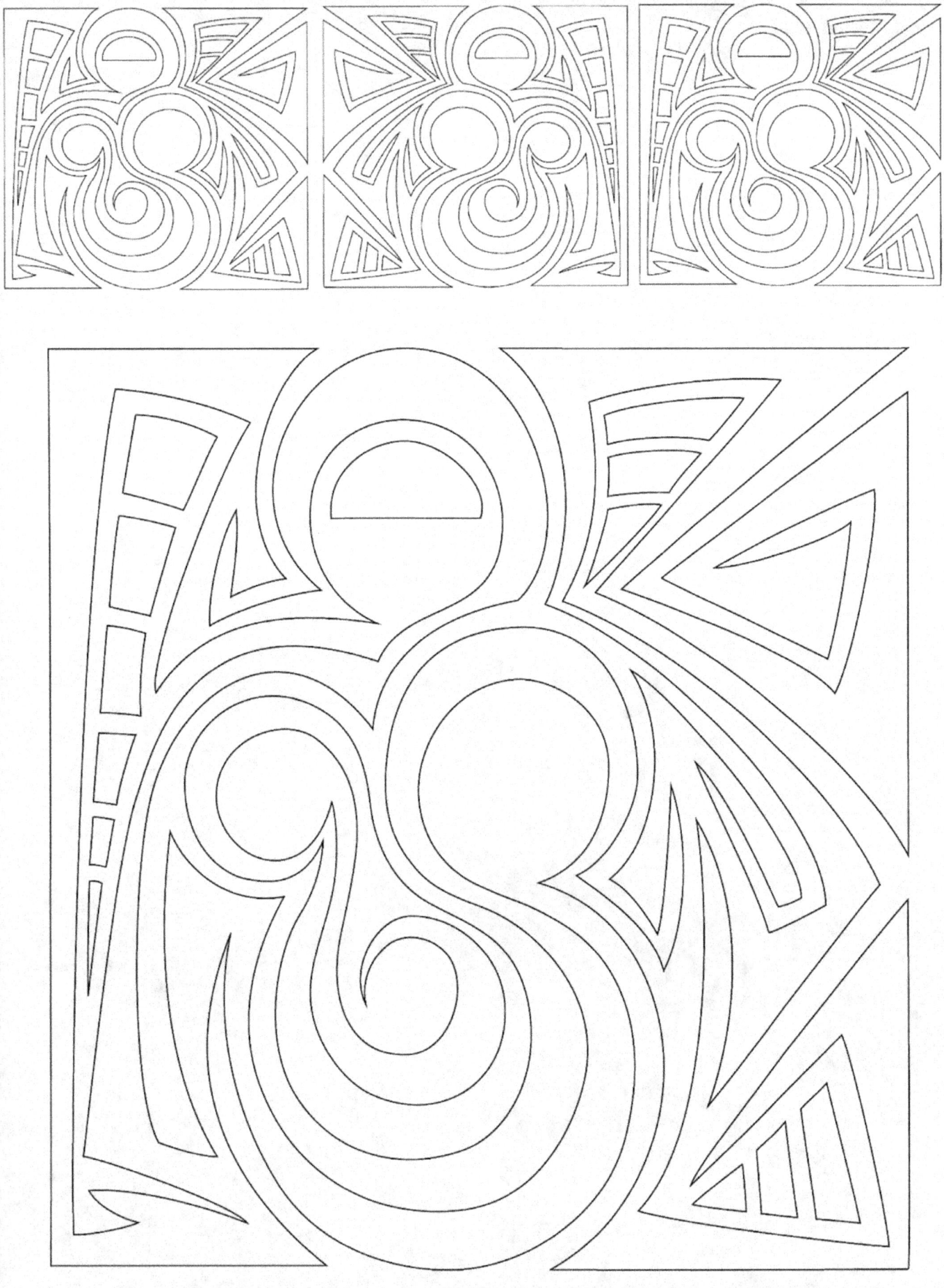

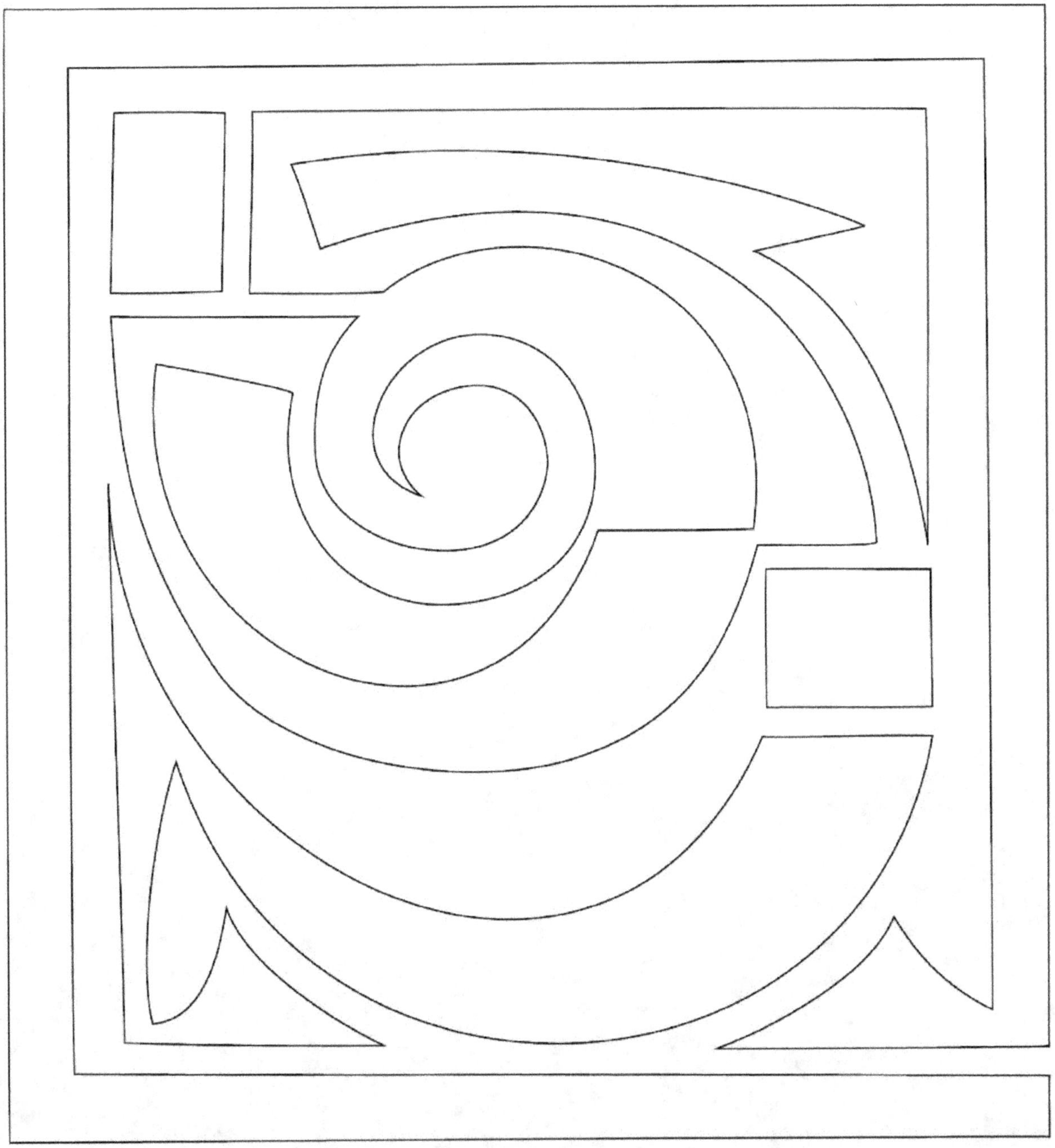

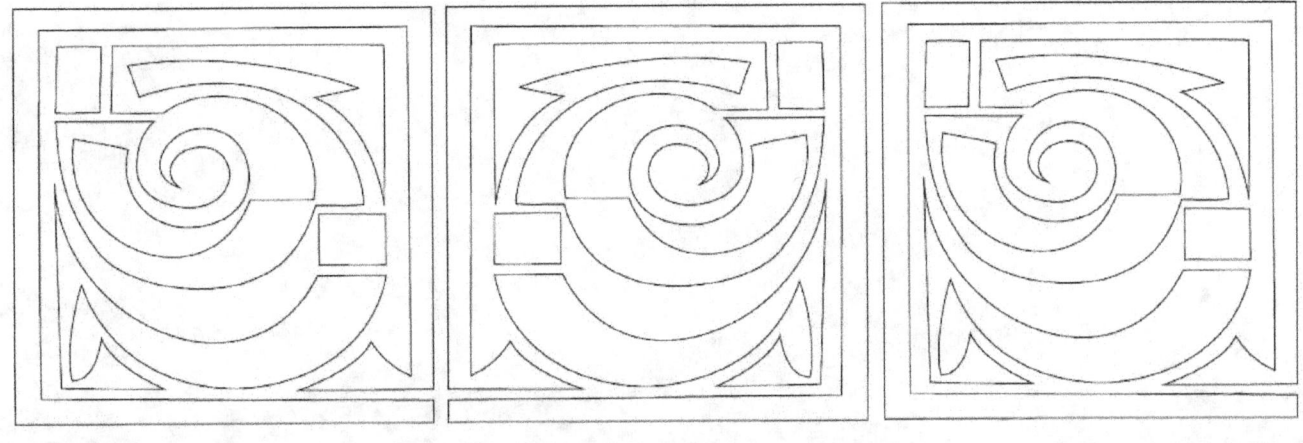

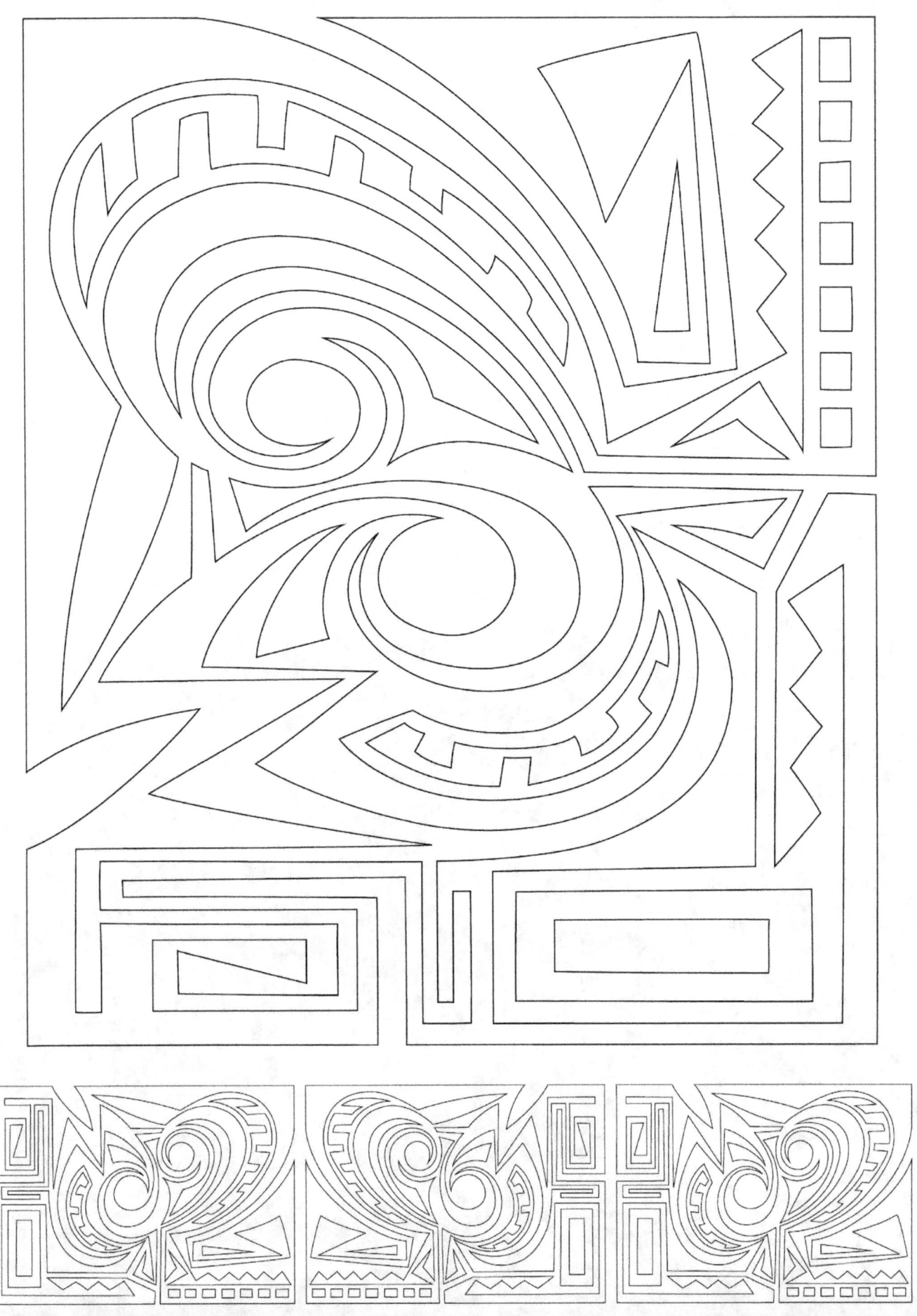

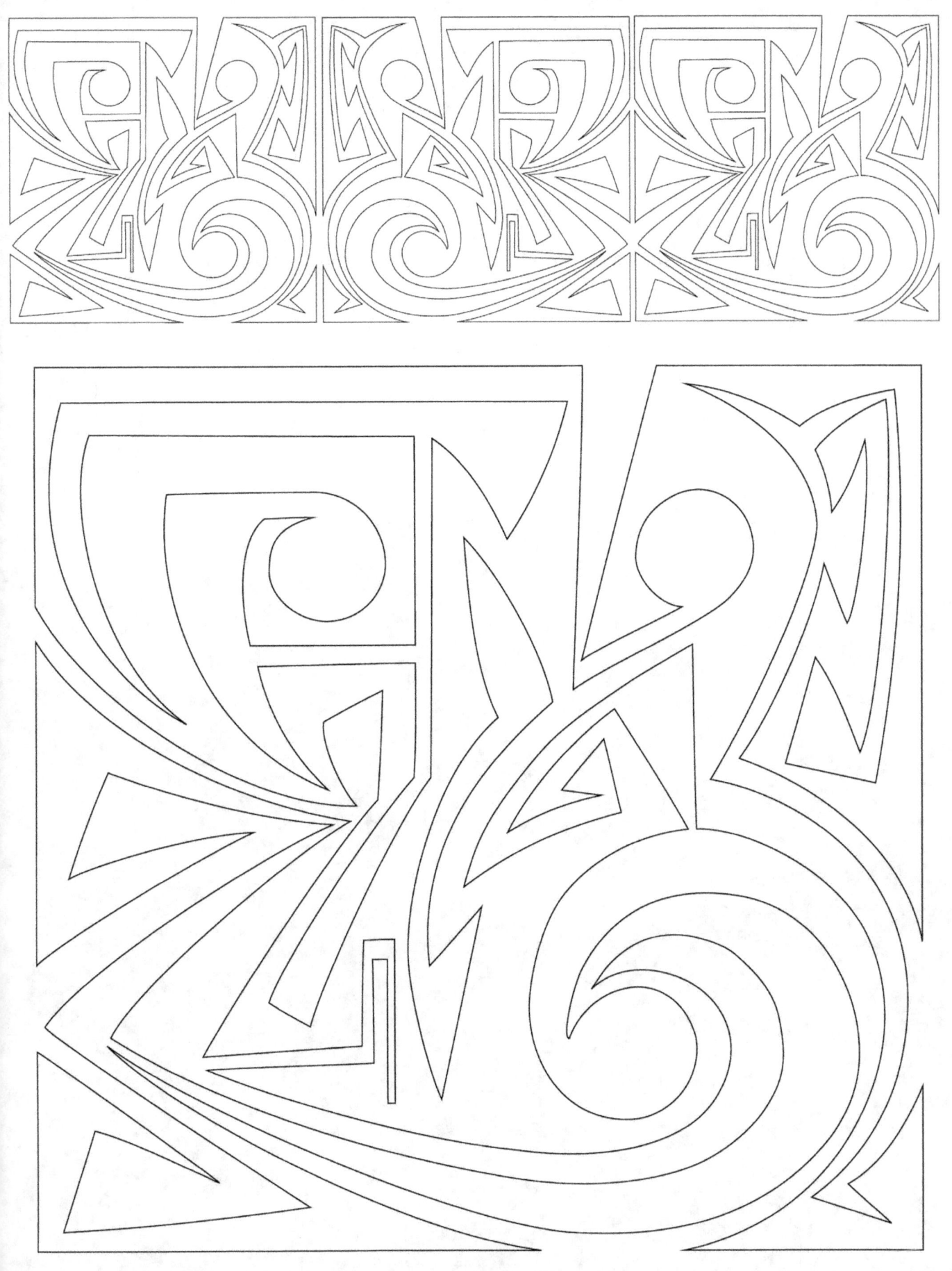

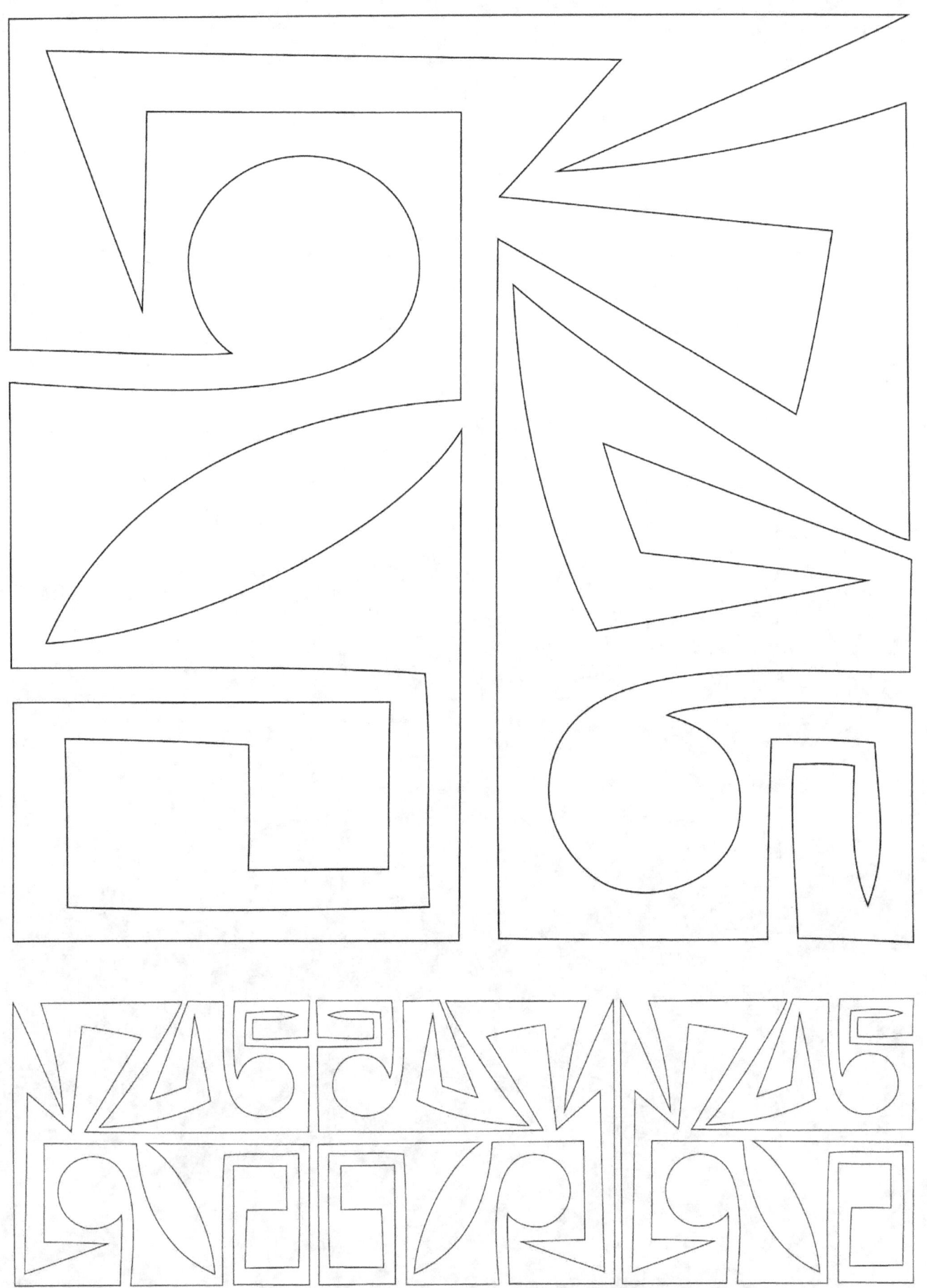

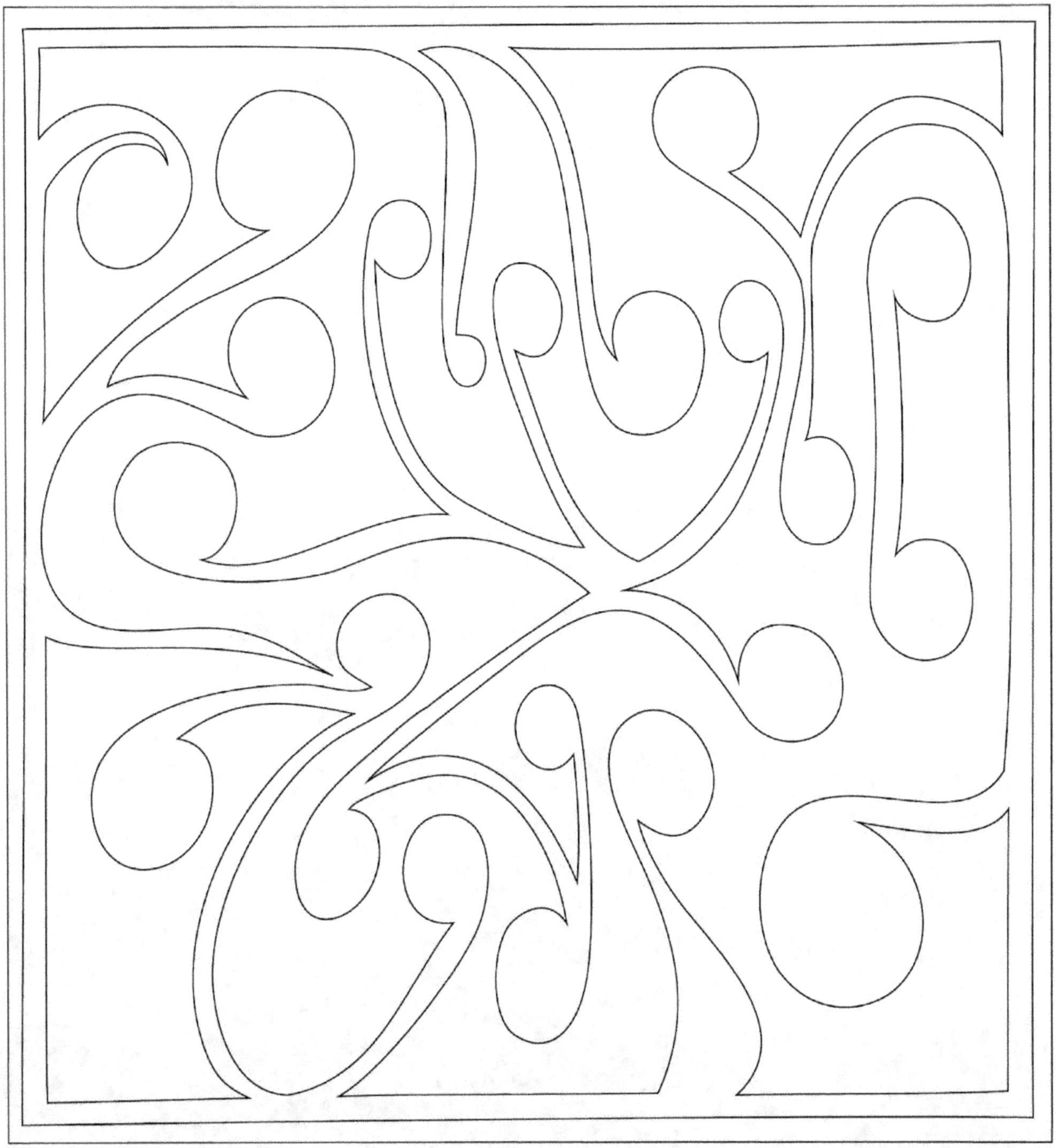

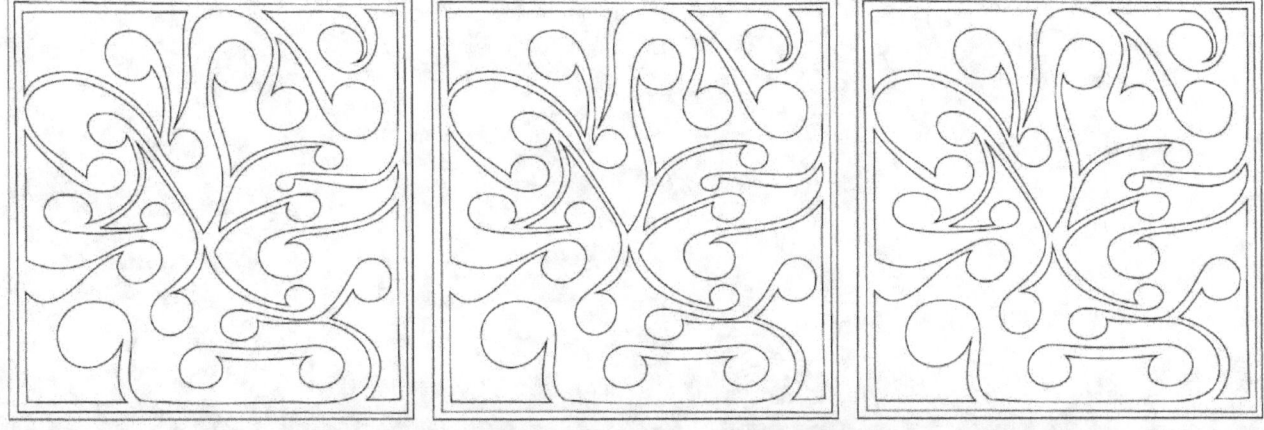

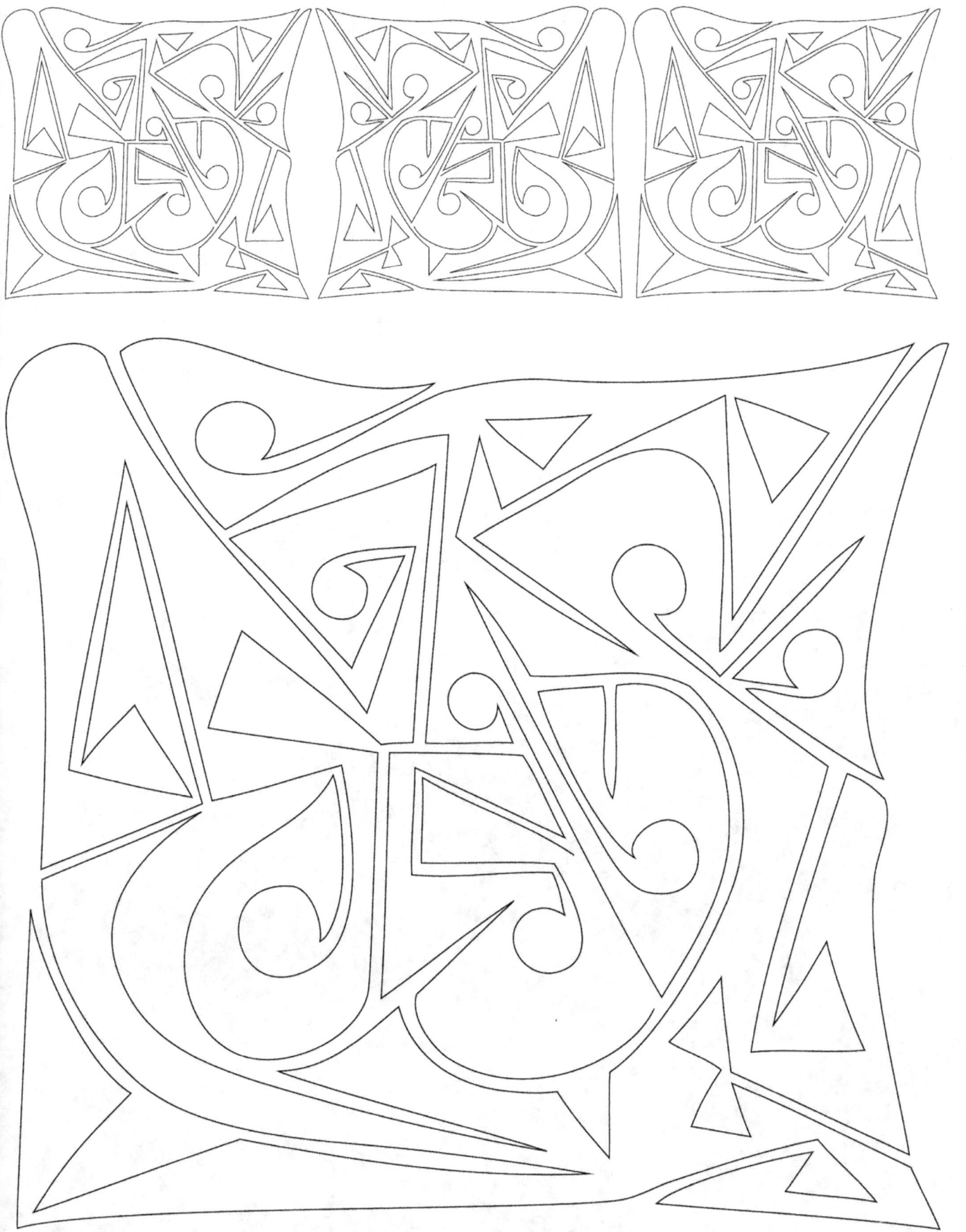

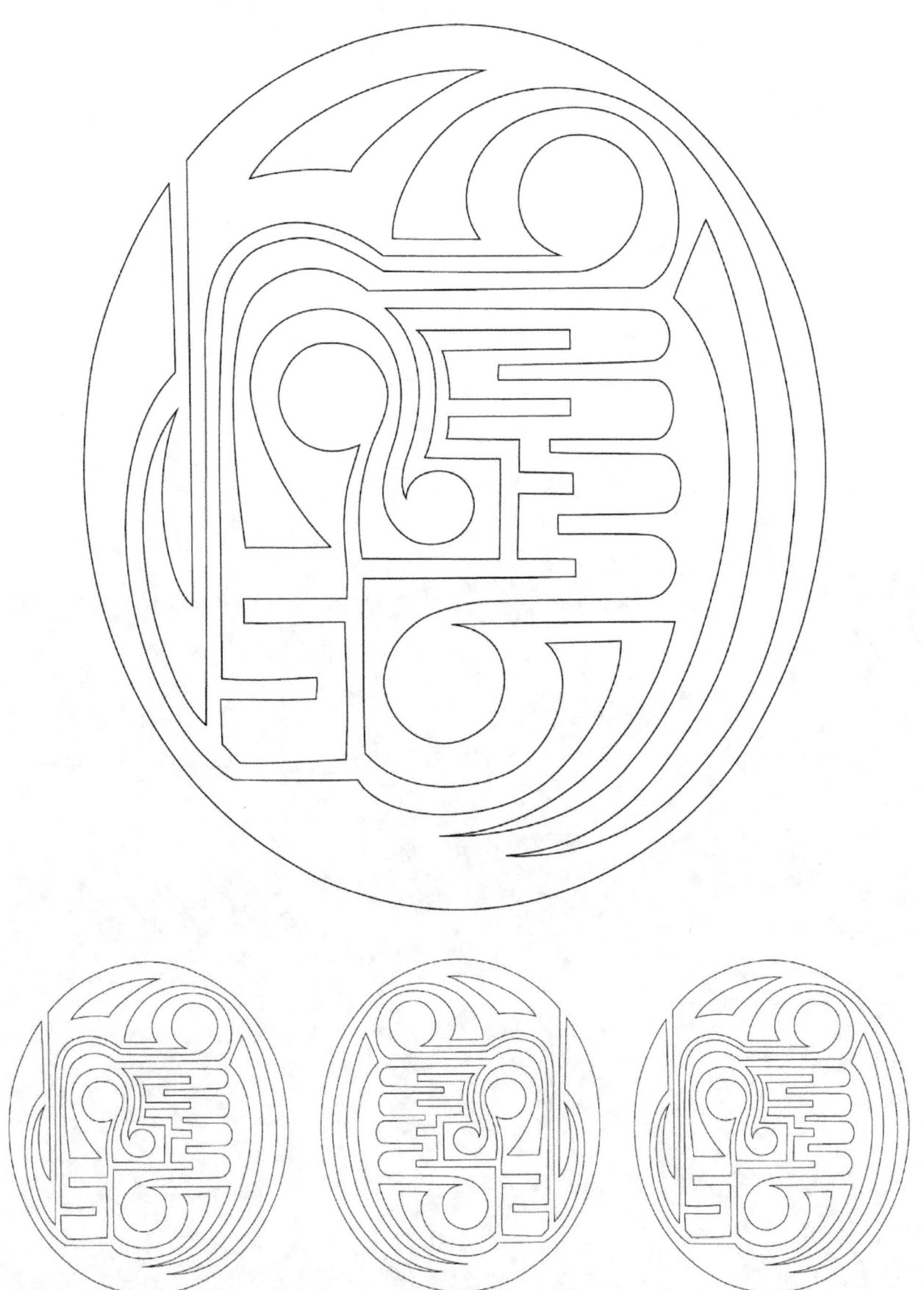

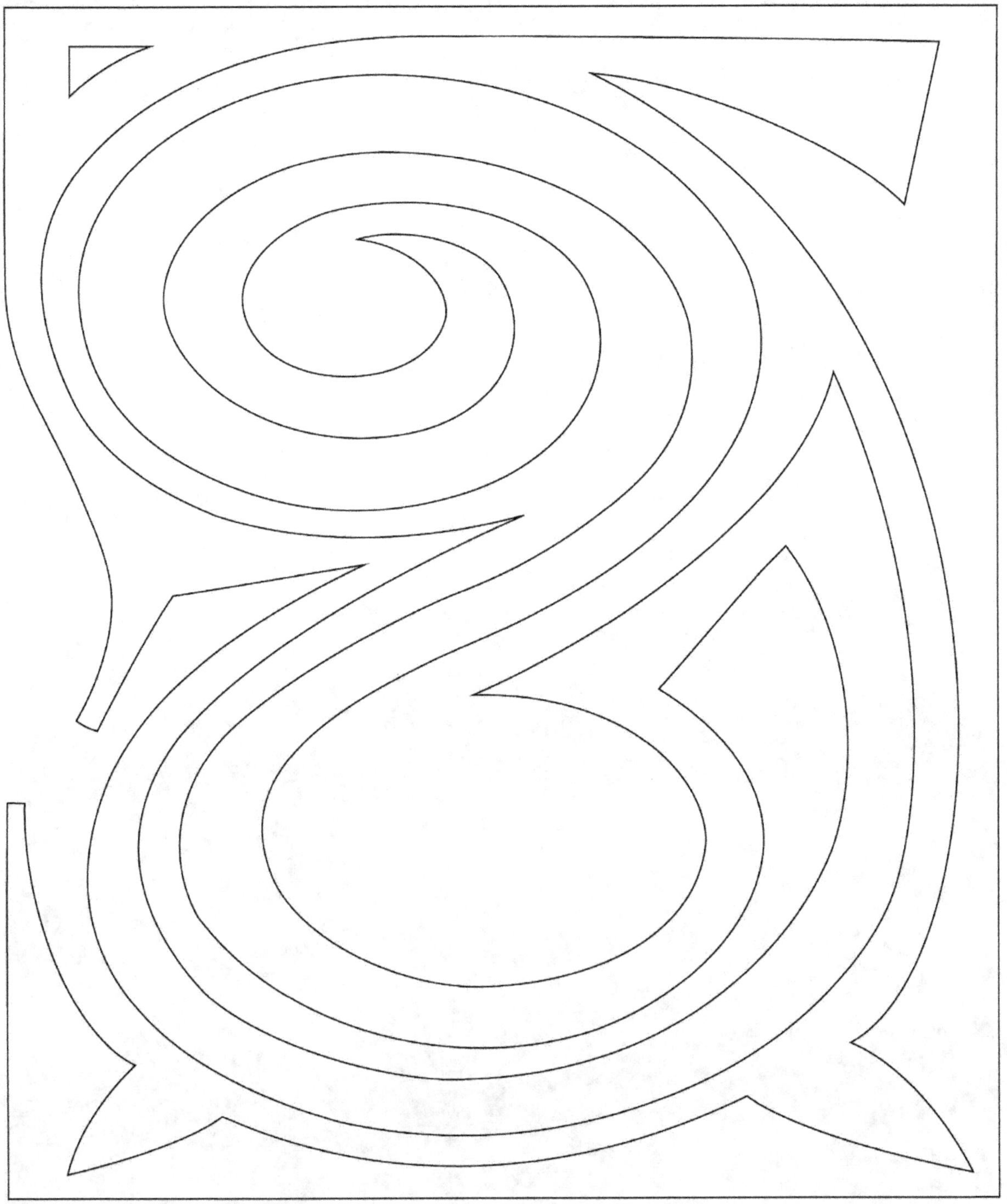

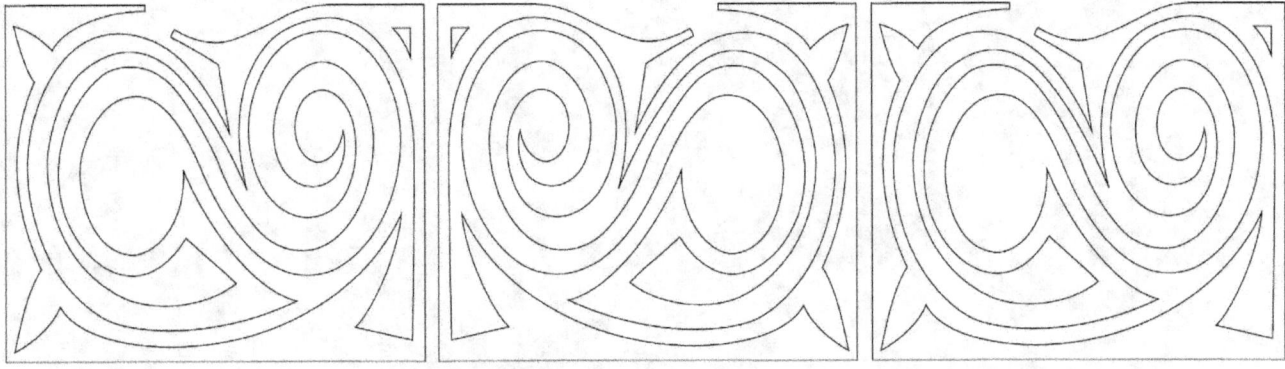

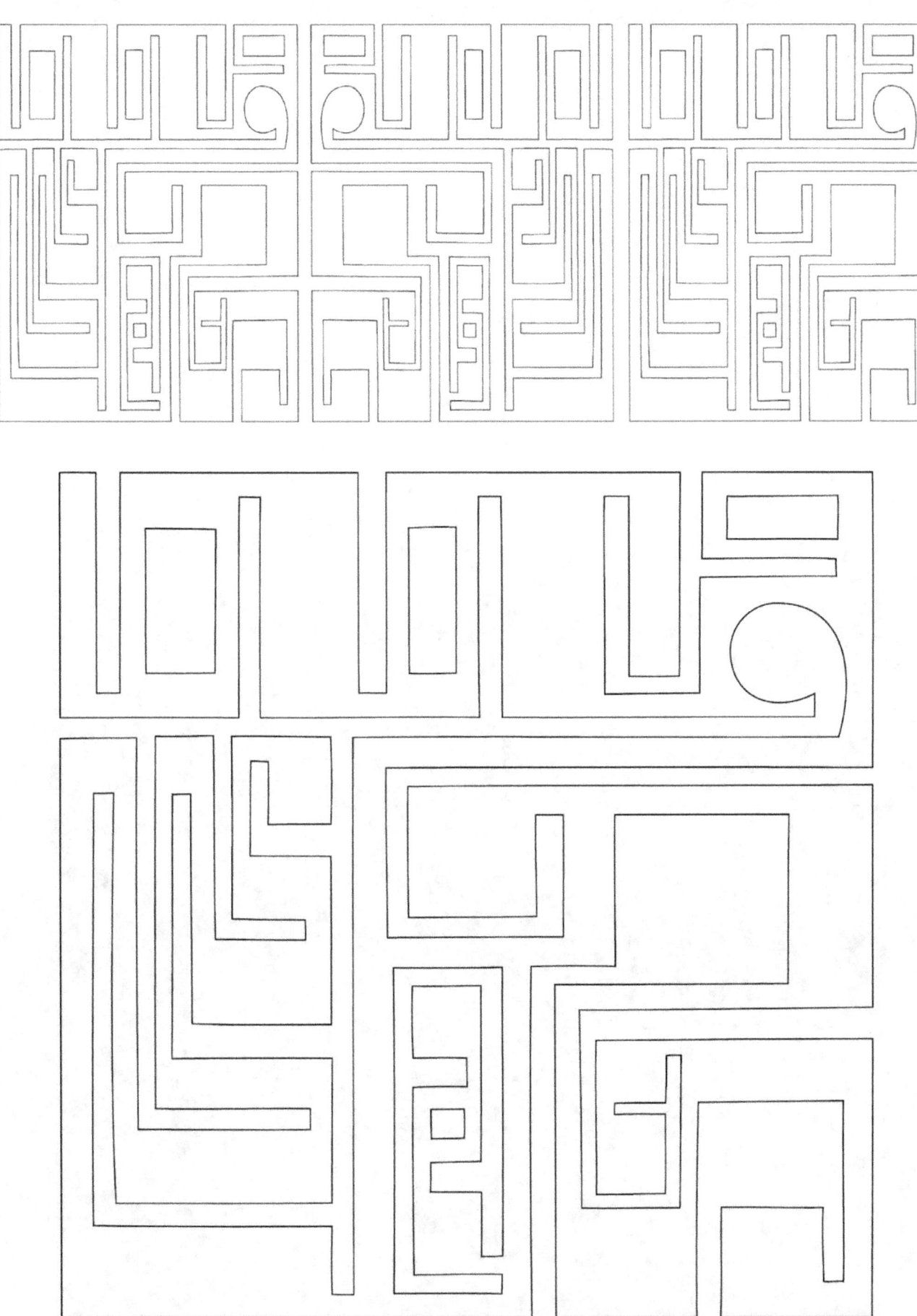

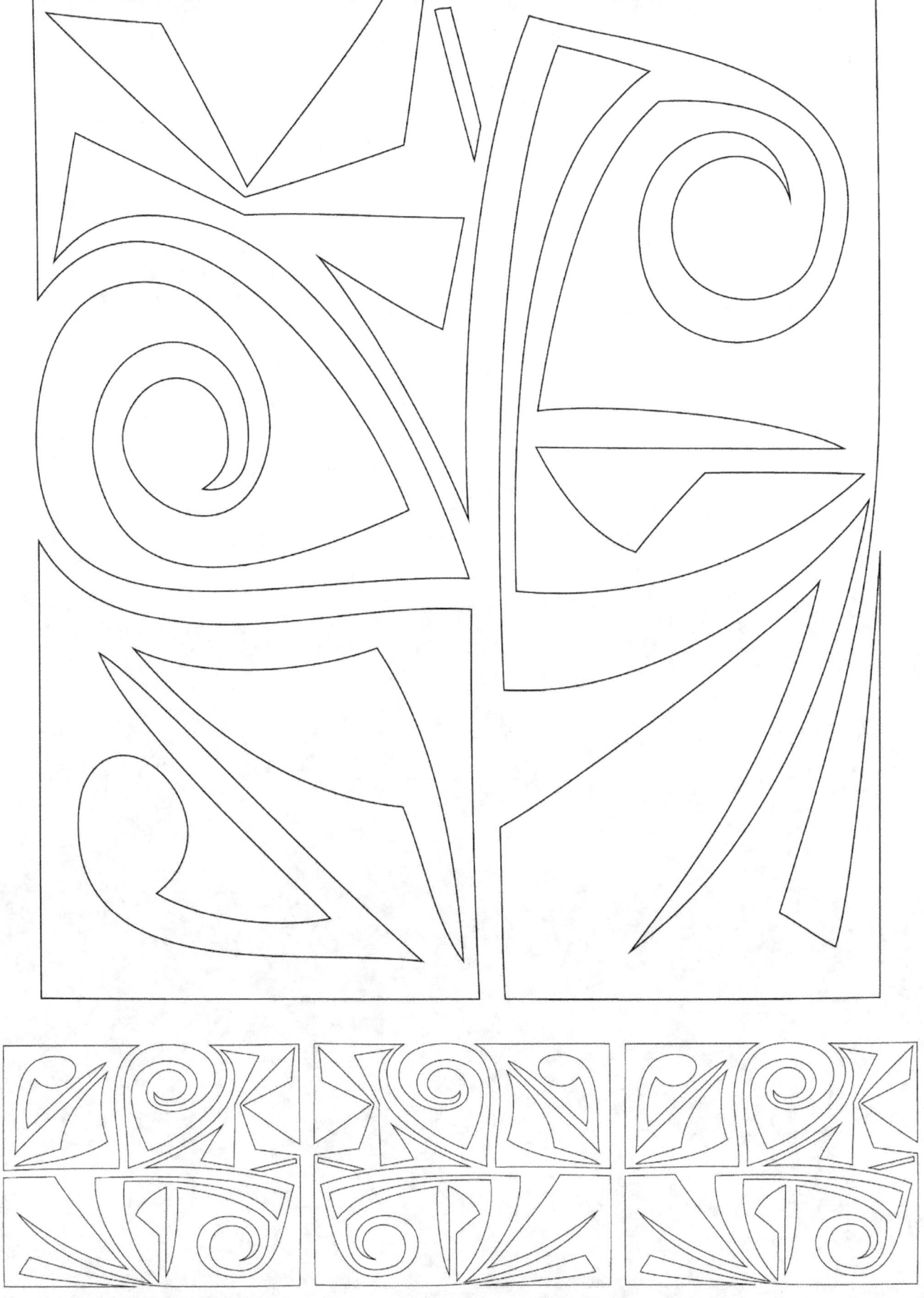

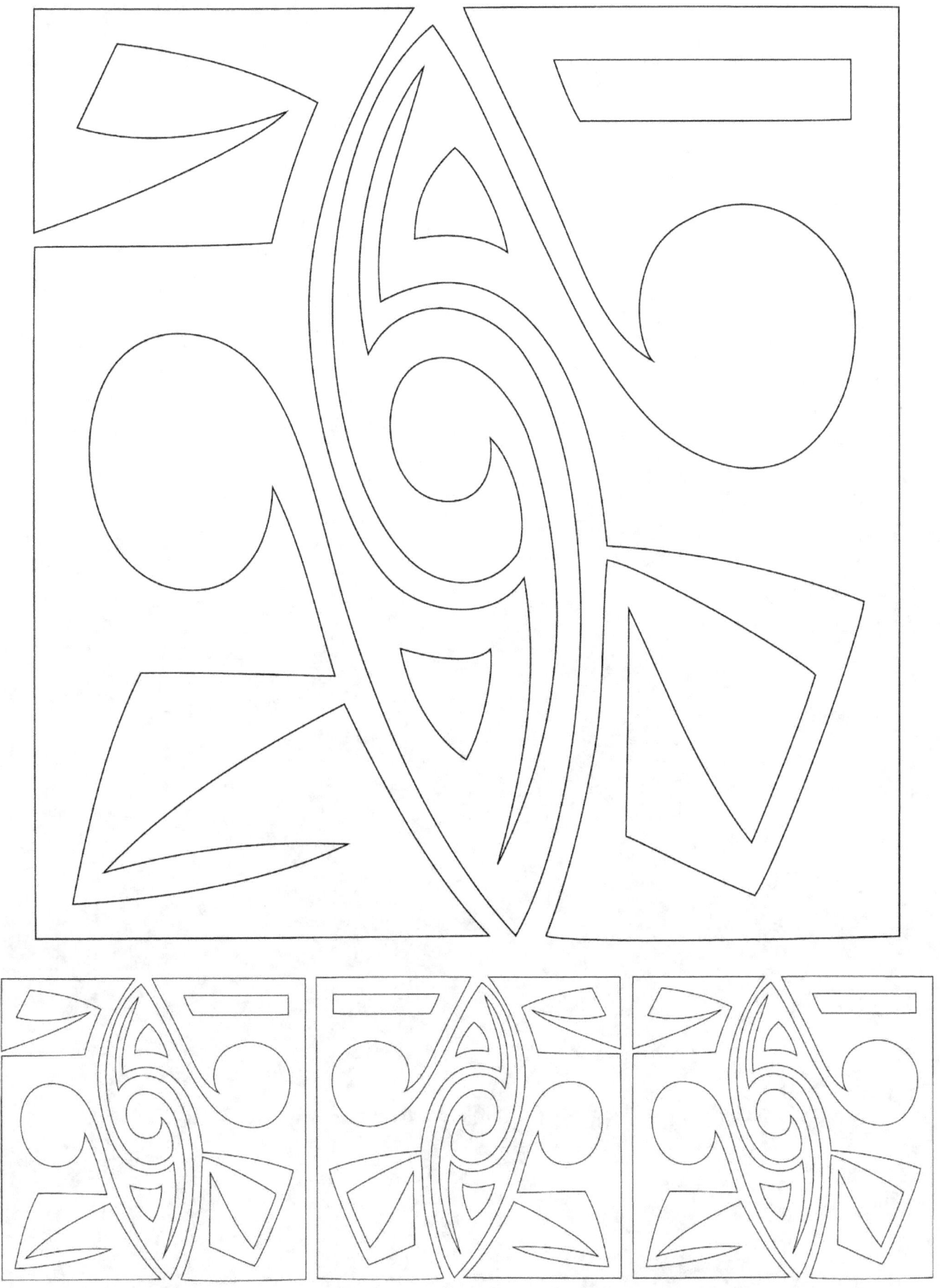

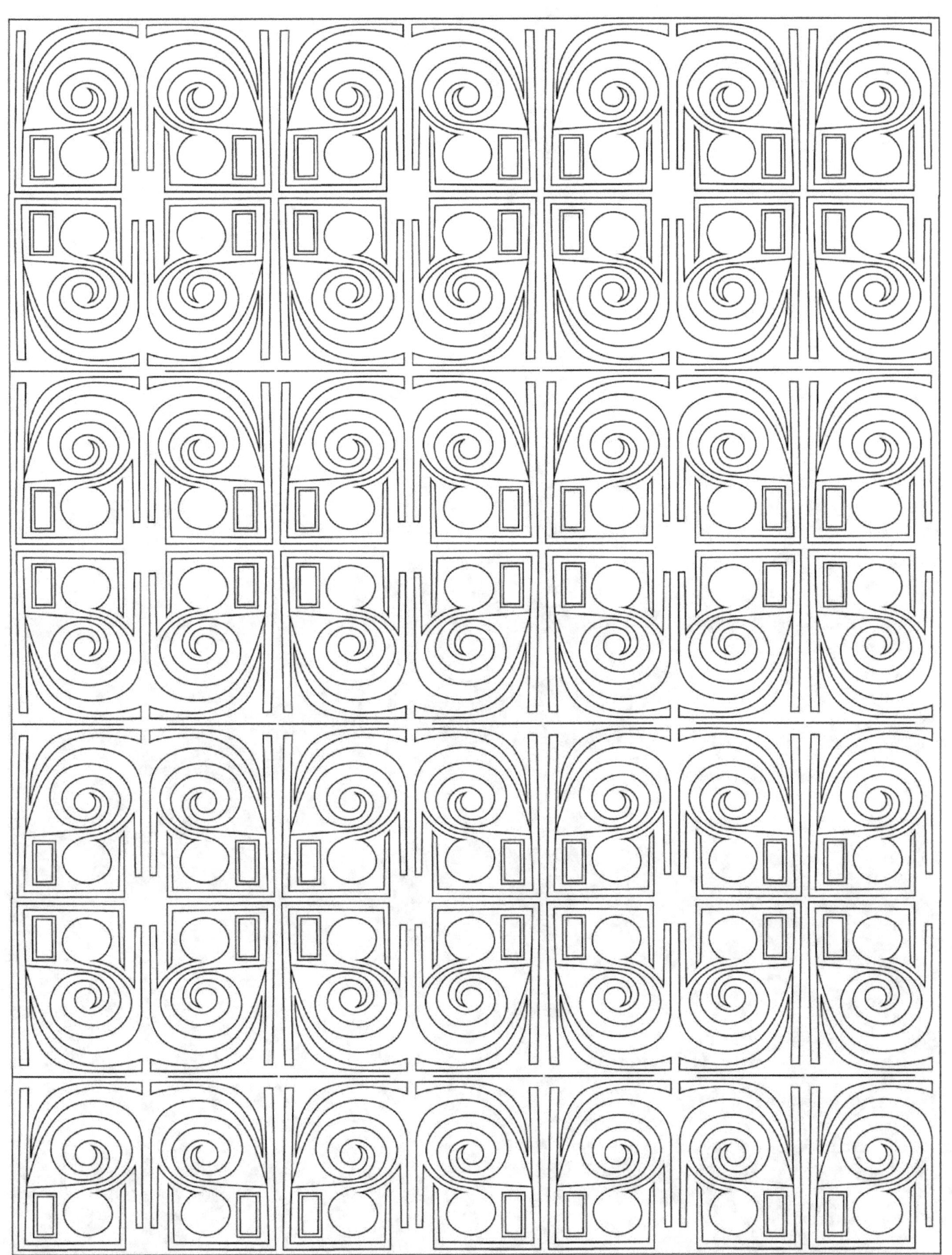

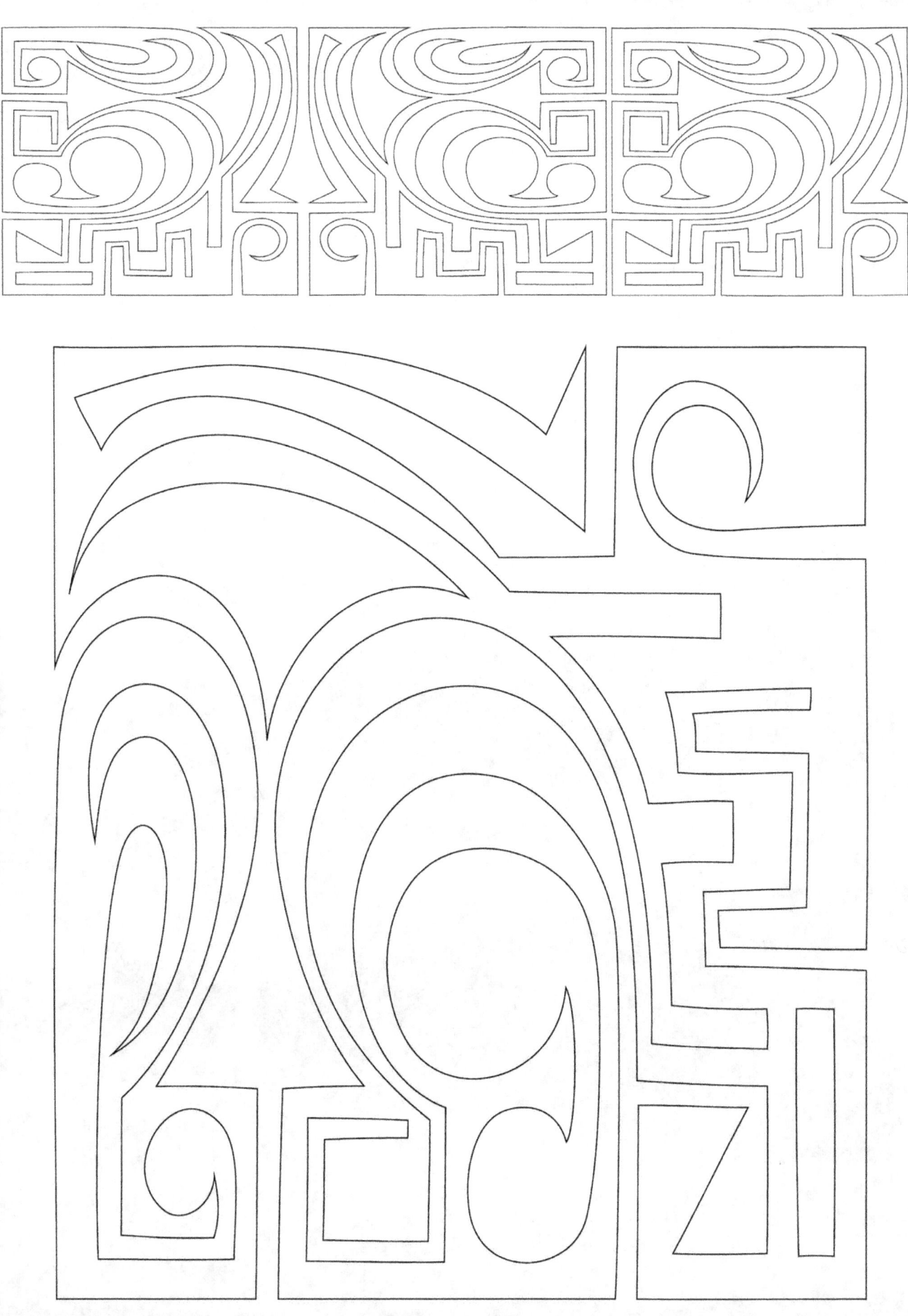

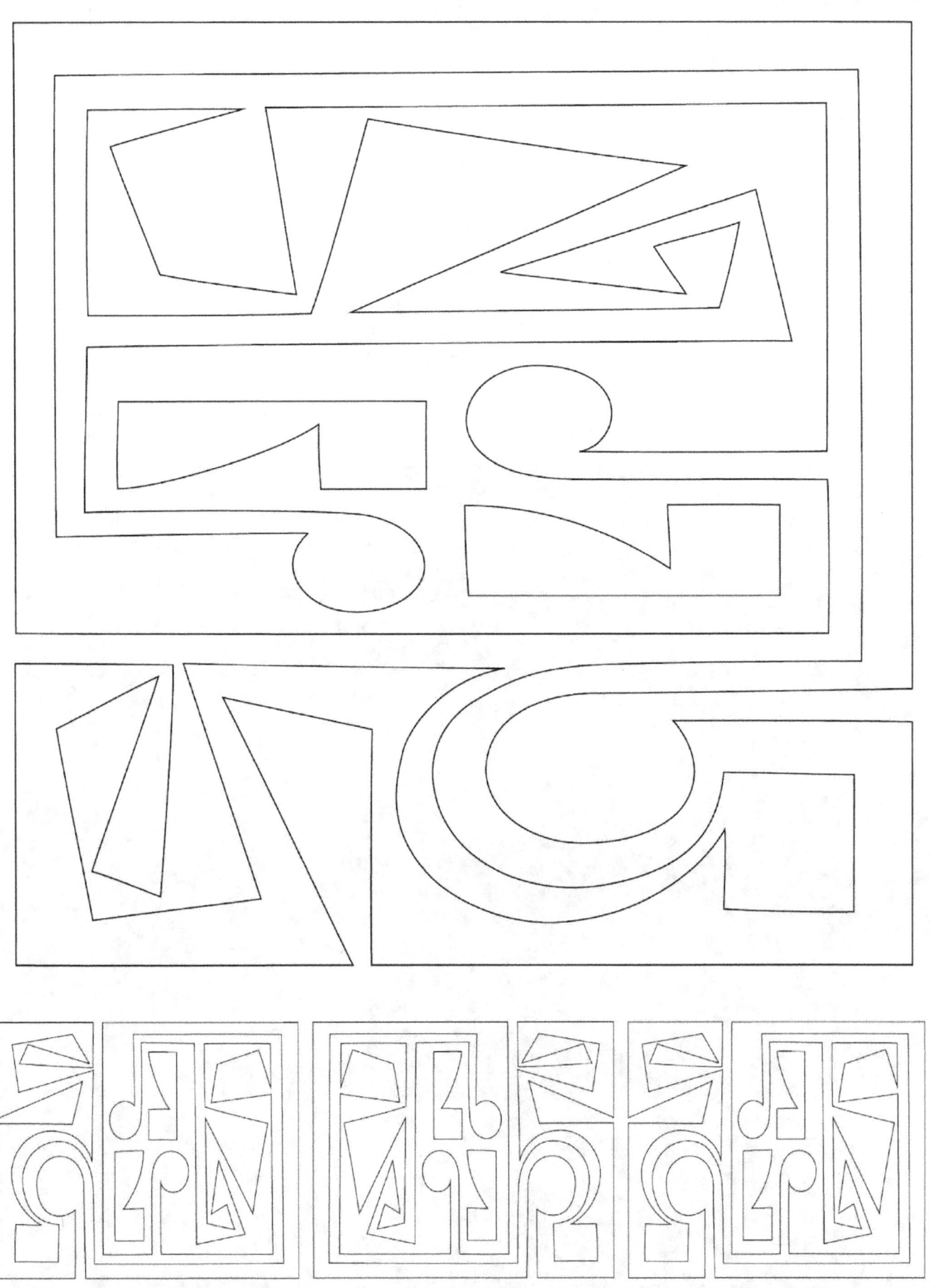

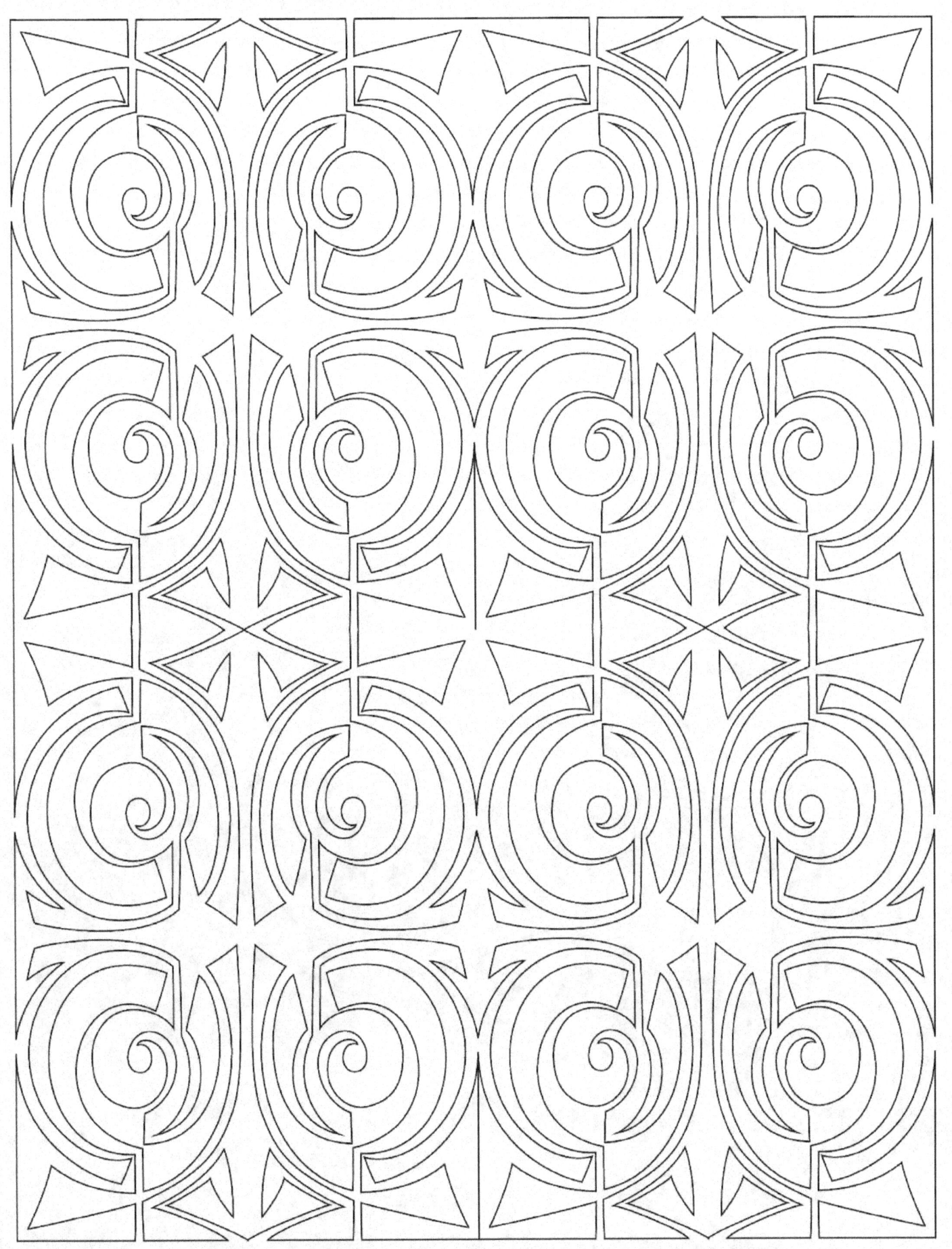

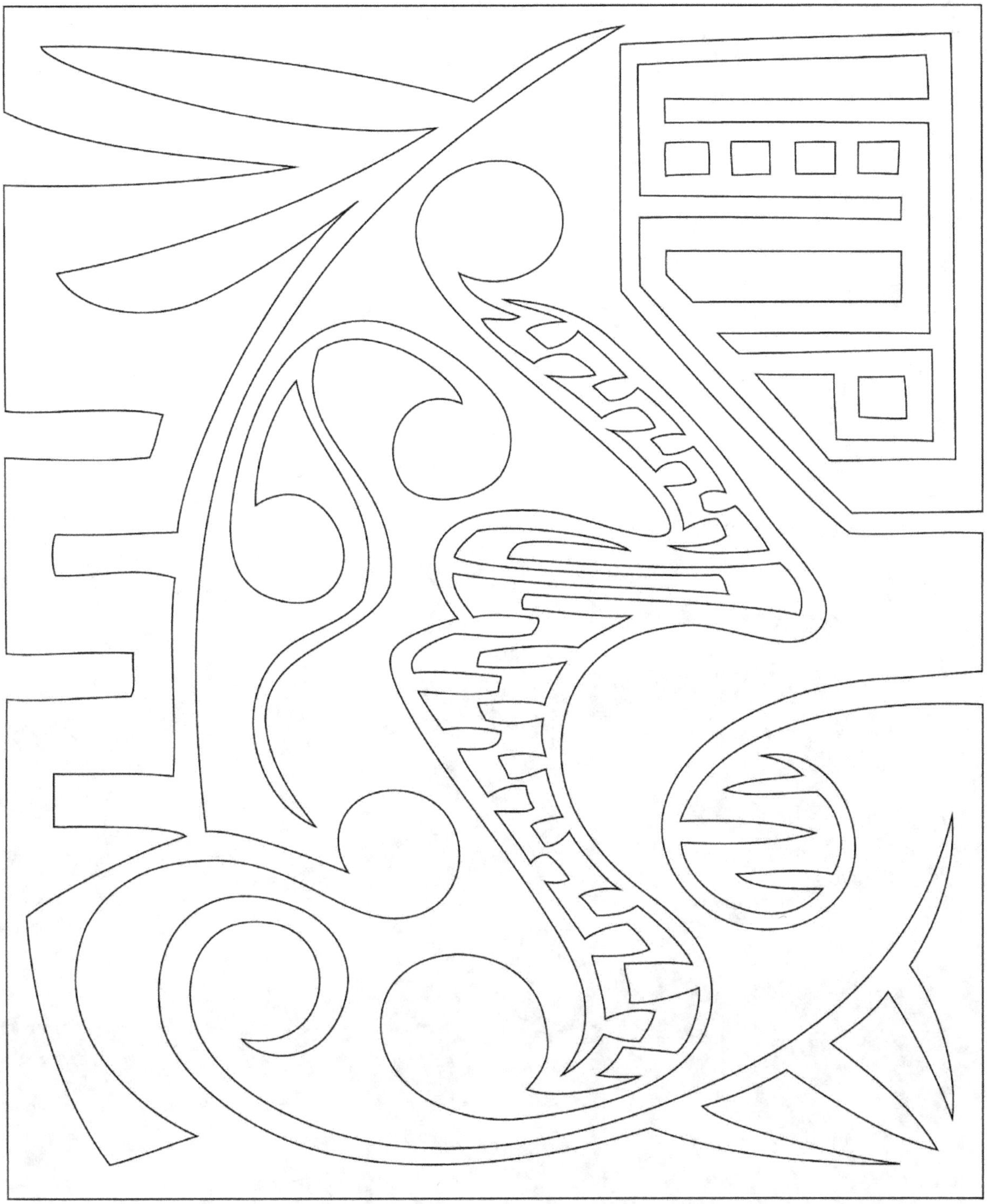

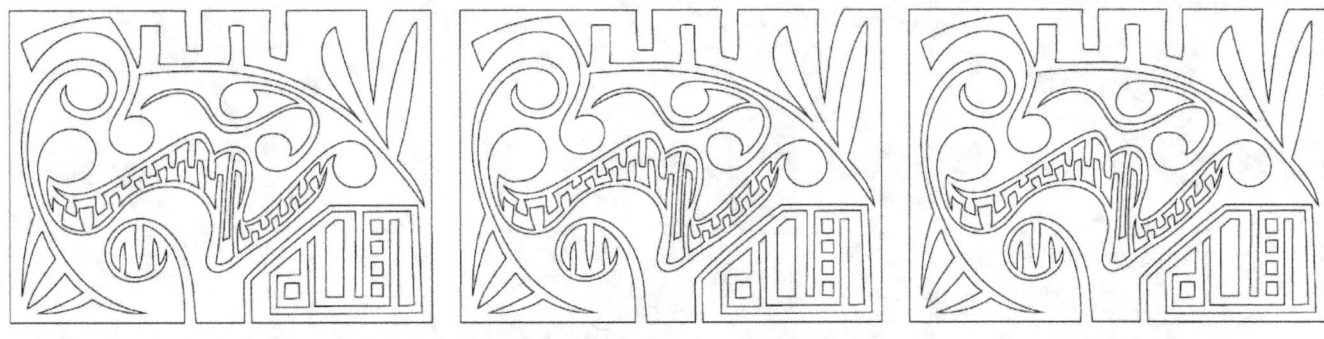

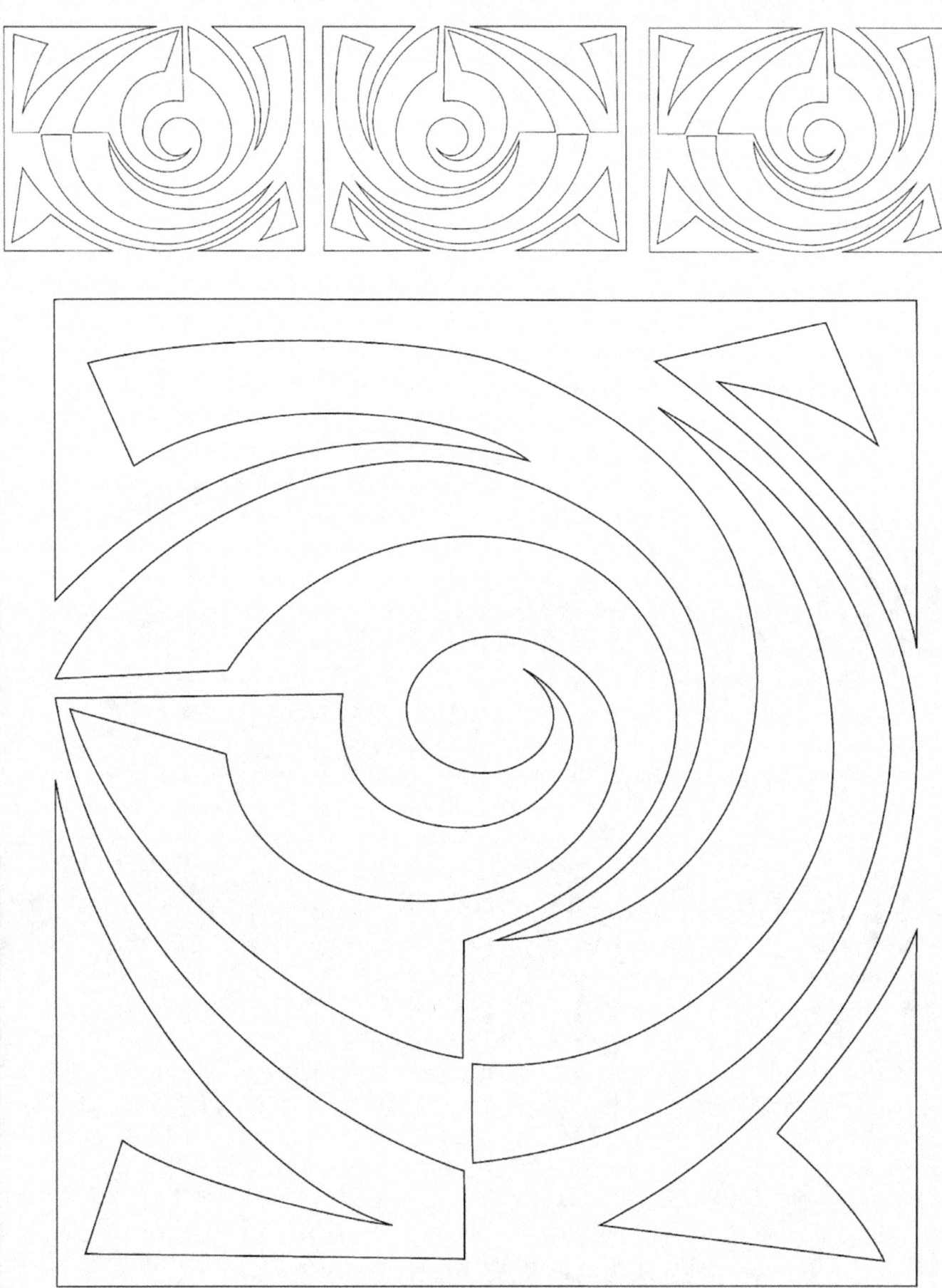

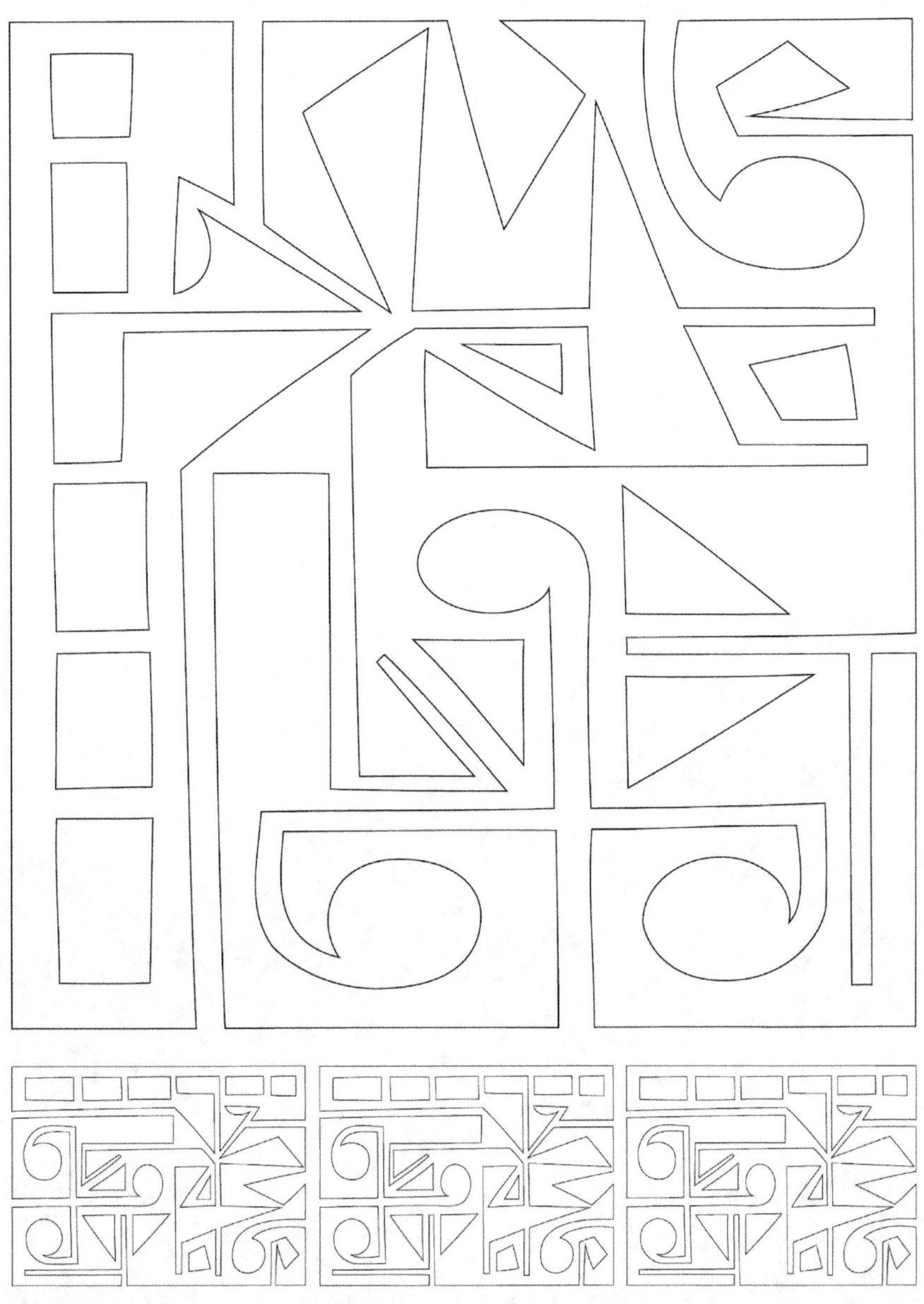

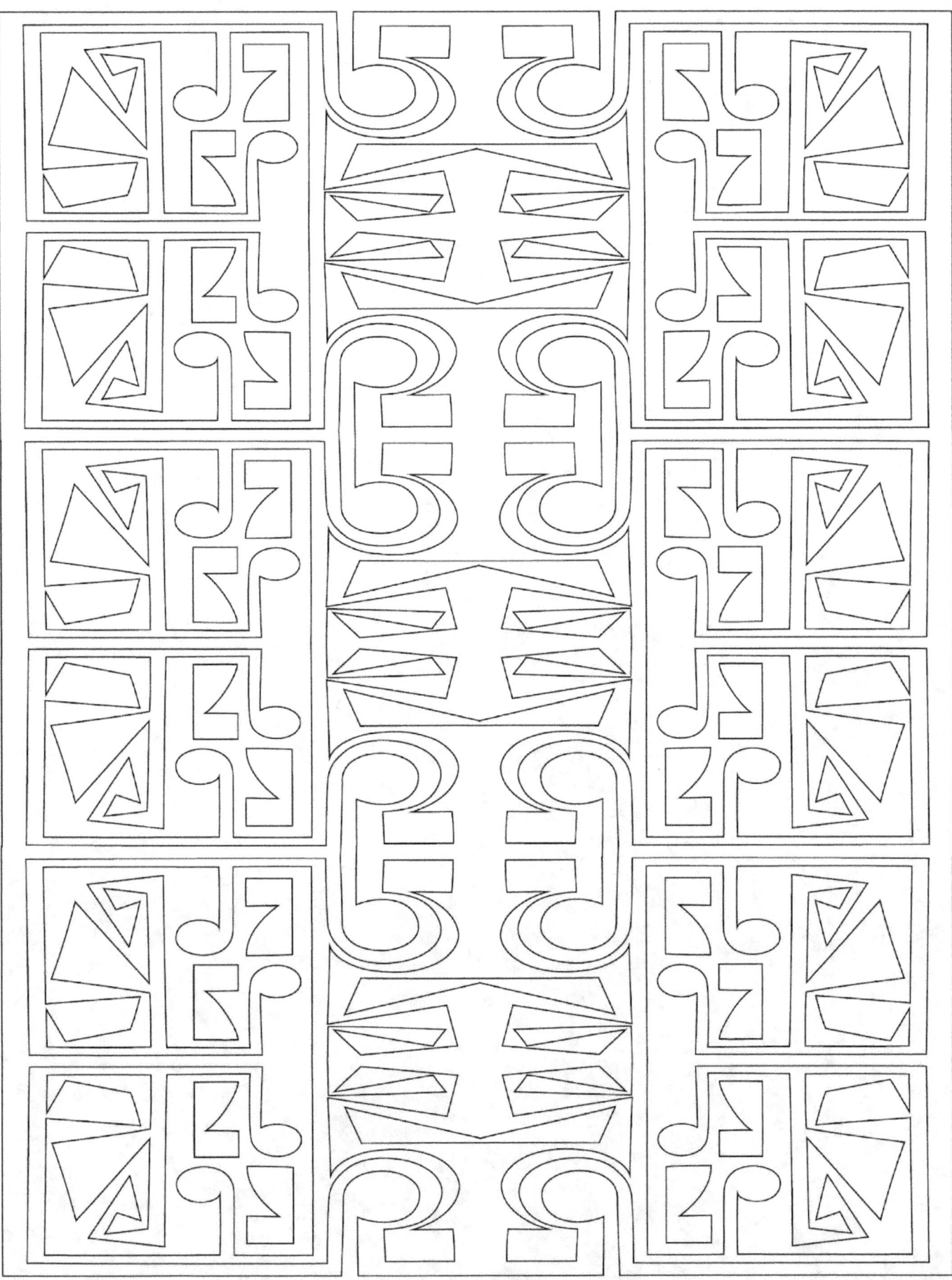

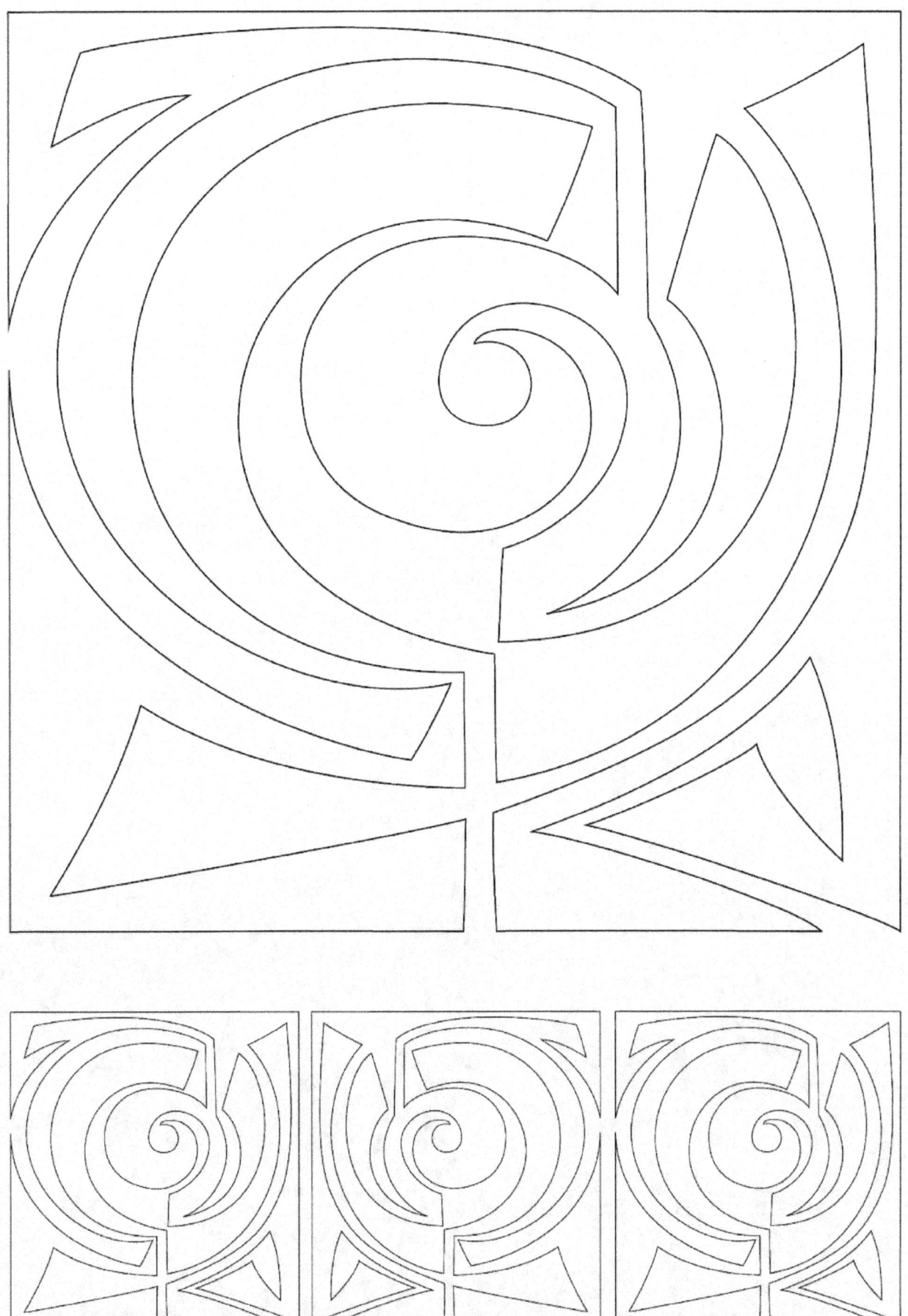

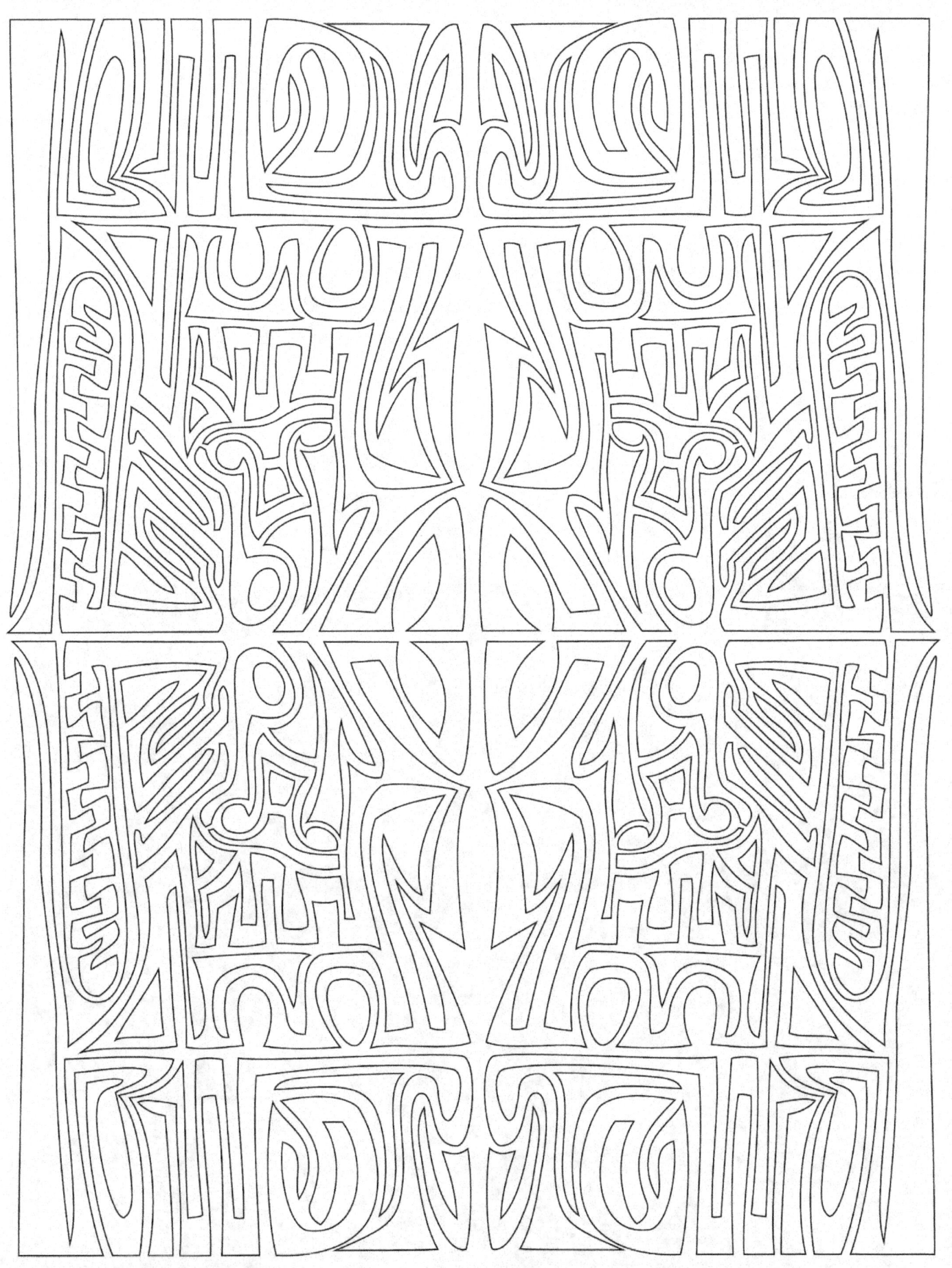

About the Author/Illustrator

Michael "Dean" Barr was born in Orlando, Florida, in July 1962. He is a retired Air Force aircraft maintainer and is currently working as a program manager for an aerospace manufacturer. He practiced his art extensively during his Air Force career, with works focusing on promoting unit morale and executing numerous commissions depicting unit aircraft from past Air Force and Marine Corps squadrons.

Dean is a listed member of the Air Force Art Program, a program that offers artists the opportunity to travel with the Air Force to locations around the world to witness military facilities and activities for the purpose of recording these events in the form of original artworks. Artists are selected from the various professional groups around the nation, such as the Societies of Illustrators in New York, Los Angeles, and San Francisco.

He currently works and lives in West Point, Utah, with his wife and best friend, Cyndi.

About the Publisher

Glass Spider Publishing is an independent publisher headquartered in Ogden, Utah. The company was founded in 2016 by author Vince Font to help bring visibility to the works of underrepresented authors and artists. Visit www.glassspiderpublishing.com to learn more.

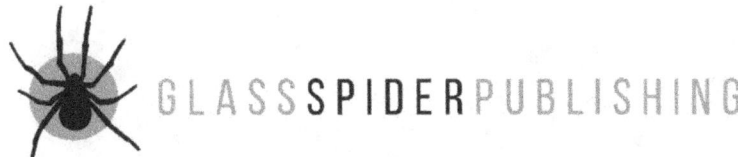

www.ingramcontent.com/pod-product-compliance
Lightning Source LLC
Chambersburg PA
CBHW080933170526
45158CB00008B/2272